Criticism in Focus

VIRGINIA WOOLF

John Mepham

Bristol Classical Press

First published in 1992 by
Bristol Classical Press
an imprint of
Gerald Duckworth & Co. Ltd
48 Hoxton Square
London N1 6PB

A catalogue for this book is available
from the British Library.

ISBN 1-85399-087-6

Printed in Great Britain by
The Cromwell Press, Melksham, Wiltshire

Contents

Introduction   1

1 Life and Career   3
  Biographical Studies   3
  Psycho-literary Speculations   13
  Critical Reception to 1965   21
  Bibliographies and Reference Works   23

2 Virginia Woolf and her Context   25
  'The Real World'   25
  Marxist Views   29
  Woolf and Psychoanalysis   32
  The Bloomsbury Group   34
  Bloomsbury Aesthetics   38

3 Virginia Woolf and Modernism   43
  Modernist Culture   43
  Modernist Forms   50

4 Feminist Studies   58
  A Passionate Audience   58
  Woolf's Feminist Theory   60
  Poststructuralist Perspectives   69
  Gender and Woolf's Novels   78
  Women's Literary Traditions   81

5 Philosophical Interpretations   87
  The Existential Project   87
  The Creative Consciousness   90
  Time, Repetition, Deconstruction   94

6 Practical and Thematic Criticism 98
   Practical Criticism 98
   Technical and Formal Analysis 100
   Themes and Theses 105

7 Editions, Drafts and Agendas 109
   The Early Novels 110
   Modernist Novels 110
   The 1930s 113
   Other Writings 115

Bibliography 119
Index 131

Introduction

Thinking, annotating, expounding goes on at a prodigious
rate all around us and over everything, like a punctual,
everlasting tide, washes the ancient sea of fiction.

('Street Haunting')

Between Virginia Woolf's death in 1941 and the mid-1970s
the number of books published about her work was quite
small. Since that time, however, there has been an enormous
flood of publications, almost impossible to keep up with.
There is now a huge amount of material, in every critical
style. There is, fortunately, no critical orthodoxy in Woolf
criticism. The 'state of the art' must be called 'pluralist', for
no one school or tendency is so dominant that it has had the
strength to overwhelm all others. Interesting and valuable
work is being written from every perspective. Long may this
remain so.

I have organized my comments on this mass of material
into divisions corresponding roughly to different styles of
criticism. There is inevitably a certain degree of arbitrariness
in this arrangement for there are books which could quite
comfortably have been included within any one of several
categories and the categories themselves could quite easily
have been different. Most of the full-length studies of Woolf's
work provide commentaries on almost all of her novels. I have
often noted just which novels are discussed in each work
because this is in itself usually an interesting indication of
the particular angle from which Woolf is being considered
therein. For a beginning student, wanting to sample the
range of different critical perspectives available, I would

recommend a starting list of some of the best or most typical books, perhaps as follows (naturally others would choose rather differently): Rose (1978), Poole (1978), Zwerdling (1986), Mepham (1991), Marcus (1988), Hussey (1986), Lee (1977), Naremore (1973), Barrett (1979). If a student then wanted to move on to a book in which Virginia Woolf is discussed from the angle of one of the more innovative and sophisticated varieties of recent critical theory, then perhaps one would point him or her in the direction of Makiko Minow-Pinkney's (1987) poststructuralist feminist treatment of her. This is a work written under the general theoretical influence of such thinkers as Lacan, Derrida and Kristeva.

For the reader who wants to know what there is to be read about some particular one of Woolf's works, there is no alternative but to begin by consulting the books listed above and the other works mentioned in my first six chapters. In addition, however, I have given in ch. 7 some more detailed and specialist information about the particular works, the early draft versions of them which are now printed, and some of the particular discussions to which they have given rise.

1

Life and Career

[handwritten: Fictional work due heavily on her life & events in it.]

Biographical Studies

More than in the case of any other writer, it is impossible to keep the literary analysis of Virginia Woolf's fiction separate from the study and interpretation of her life. Many readers have found that they want to turn to her life story as a response to reading her novels. This may be in part because the worlds created in her fictions more than commonly overlap with the world of her own experience. Her novels consistently draw on her life for their central episodes and characters. They rework her bereavements, her madness, her obsessions, and so on. Many of her novels contain characters who can be read as partial self-portraits. For Woolf, writing was a form of self-exploration or even self-creation.

At many points, however, the novels are very guarded or reticent on what seem to be central, determining influences and issues in her characters' lives, as if they are hiding essential evidence or fearful of stepping into crucial but radically unsettling areas of experience. It has been argued that there is a consistent pattern in the process of composition of each of her novels. Earlier, draft versions are usually more revealing or unguarded than the published versions. The drafts display crucial emotions, for example, anger, feminist resentments against men, sexual desires, fears and confusions, which are then covered over again in the final rewriting. (See the Preface in Ginsberg and Gottlieb.)

Perhaps as a result of this, many readers have felt the desire
to turn from the novels to the biographical and autobiographical writings. Moreover, it may be that readers have felt
that the mysterious processes of artistic creativity might, in
this case, yield up their secrets, since, in this particular
artist's life, her disturbance and impulse were so very near
the surface of her mind and are so graphically recorded in
her private papers.

Goldensohn (1987), surveying many of the life studies and
autobiographical writings to which I will refer below, specu-
lates that it is as if readers were hoping that acquaintance
with Woolf's private papers would allow them to get back to
the authentic point of origin of the fictions, to find in the
disturbance of Woolf's life and mind the origin of her imaginative genius. She argues, however, that the Virginia Woolf
who is disclosed in her diaries and letters had many unap-
pealing features. She was xenophobic, at times racist, often
snobbish and contemptuous of ordinary people's efforts, and
damagingly over-fastidious in her reactions to other writers'
work. In her intimate relationships she was frequently infantile. The diaries and letters can occasionally make painful
reading. It is, says Goldensohn, like finding a classical statue
defaced by a moustache, though one drawn on by the subject
herself. However, it may be that it is a relief to discover all
her confusion of attitude and untidiness of emotion, for
perhaps this counterbalances something too orderly, too rigorously controlled in her novels? Goldensohn's perceptive
article raises subtle questions about the relationship between Woolf's artistic creativity and other aspects of her life
and personality and ponders on the common experience of
many of her readers, which is the blurring of boundaries
between fiction and non-fiction, so that we read the novels
with the diaries in hand and cannot keep the different worlds
entirely distinct. What we discover, Goldensohn argues, is
that Woolf's fiction is constrained by a damaging decorum, a
panicky impulse to conceal certain painful material, so that
it is only when we read it in conjunction with her more
revealing private writings that we can imaginatively reas-
semble and appreciate the dispersed wholeness of her

remarkable personality.

It was the publication of Woolf's private papers which made this blurring of boundaries possible. The process was initiated in 1953 when Leonard Woolf published *A Writer's Diary*, a one-volume selection of passages from the thirty manuscript volumes of her diary. He chose passages which threw light particularly on the process of conception and composition of her novels. In addition, we are also given many fascinating glimpses of the Woolfs' marriage and social life and of her illnesses, collapses and the background to her suicide. Yet more information on all these topics, as well as about the Woolfs' work together at the Hogarth Press, the history of their relations with the Bloomsbury Group and their place in the general cultural and political currents of their time, was given in the volumes of Leonard Woolf's autobiography.

The next major turning point came with the publication of the two-volume biography of Virginia Woolf by her nephew Quentin Bell in 1972. Bell could draw not only on his personal acquaintance with his aunt and many of her family and friends, but also on many unpublished private documents. The situation in Woolf studies changed dramatically through the 1970s and 1980s as many of these papers were edited and published. Her *Diary*, meticulously edited and annotated by Anne Olivier Bell and Andrew McNeillie, considered by many to be a major literary work in its own right, was published in five volumes between 1977 and 1984. Six volumes of her *Letters* have also been published. A useful addition to these volumes is *The Letters of Vita Sackville-West to Virginia Woolf*, edited by Louise DeSalvo and Mitchell Leaska, which has an informative introduction.

On his death in 1969 Leonard Woolf deposited his own and many of his wife's papers with the University of Sussex Library. Many other papers and manuscripts have found their way to the Berg Collection of the New York Public Library. Among the Monks House Papers at Sussex, several autobiographical pieces by Virginia Woolf were discovered. These included Memoir Club papers, a 1908 memoir called 'Reminiscences' and, most importantly, her 'Sketch of the

Past'. This very fine piece of writing, an exploration of her life as a child and young woman, was written in the years immediately before her death in 1941. These papers were published as *Moments of Being* in 1976. 'A Sketch of the Past' is one of the main sources of information about those episodes in her early life which have so fascinated the psychobiographers: the deaths of her mother and half-sister (in 1895 and 1897) and the sexual abuse which she suffered as a child.

Many draft versions of her novels have now also been published (see ch. 7). Finally, Virginia Woolf was a prolific essayist and to this day essays by her, published anonymously in *The Times Literary Supplement*, are still being discovered. The first three volumes of *The Essays of Virginia Woolf* have now been published (there will be six volumes eventually). In ch. 7 I give some information about the many earlier volumes of her essays. Fifty years after her death, we are now approaching the end of the publication of Woolf's papers. Most recently her early diaries and essays, dating from 1897 to 1909, have been published, edited by Mitchell Leaska, in *A Passionate Apprentice* (1990). However, as her novels come out of copyright in Britain in 1992, plans have already been made to begin a whole new round of publishing activity, to produce scholarly editions of her novels.

So the reader interested in the biographical background to Woolf's work now has available a vast amount of published material to which to refer. The starting point, apart from her own writings, would be the 1972 Quentin Bell biography which, in spite of its limitations, is established as an indispensable point of reference. It is, moreover, a pleasure to read. It is beautifully written, elegant and witty. Quentin Bell's work is graced with an unfailing amiability and an impressively good temper which he miraculously seldom loses in print even after what is now nearly two decades of rather aggressive criticism from some quarters. The strengths of his book are the detail with which he reconstructed Woolf's family life, her marriage and her relations with her sister and her friends. It was this book that first alerted people to the episodes of sexual abuse to which she was subject as an adolescent, though on this, as on most topics, Bell refrains from speculation on their significance or their long-term effects.

The general picture of Woolf that we derive from Bell is that of a fragile woman, constantly vulnerable to mental disturbance, unfailingly and effectively supported and managed by her husband. Her close and dependent relationship with her sister Vanessa (Quentin Bell's mother) is also stressed. What is missing from this portrait is any sense that Virginia Woolf was an intelligent and thoughtful woman. Bell stresses the fantastic rather than the thoughtful qualities of her mind. Apart from her madness, Woolf's inner life has little place in his book. Above all, he omits any detailed consideration of that activity which occupied more of her life than any other – her writing. He does not draw on his knowledge of the details of her life to ask why she wrote, or why she wrote in the ways that she did, or what her writings meant to her. Her work is present in this story only in its externals and not as an aspect of her personality or as the activity which kept her on an even keel for most of her life.

Gindin (1981) says in criticism of Bell that 'Virginia Woolf is interesting precisely because she could manifest a self in fiction that she could not always manage in ordinary experience.' Bell's biography is insubstantial, he argues, because it fails to draw on the fiction, and is therefore insensitive to those reverberations of the self that only come through in the fiction. Michael Holroyd (1976) and Ellen Hawkes (1974) both point to the fact that Bell's view of Woolf is an external one. The consequence of Bell's refusal of literary and psychological interpretation is that we do not feel what it was like to be Virginia Woolf, says Holroyd. Bell's attitude is one of 'watchful protectiveness', which may be appropriate in a nephew but is misguided in a biographer. Ellen Hawkes says that we are left with the figure of a neurotic virgin, rather than a woman who positively valued chastity. Moreover, it is impossible to discuss Woolf as a woman without discussing her as a writer, because for her, writing was a continual investigation of her own identity and personal development.

Bell's sternest critics have been the psychobiographers

and the feminists. Of the former, see particularly Roger
Poole, who focuses on Bell's assessment of Woolf's relations
with her husband and on the account he gives of her mental
ill-health. Bell does not hesitate to refer to Virginia Woolf, as
she did herself, as 'mad' or 'insane', and he sees Leonard's
role in managing her madness in an unambiguously positive
light. It is his uncritical use of these categories and his
emphasis on Leonard's benign role that are most emphatically challenged by Poole.

Leonard Woolf remarked that his wife was the least political animal since Aristotle invented the term and Bell goes
along with this view. She is seen as a comic incompetent when
it comes to organized political activity and she is not taken
seriously where her own political writings are concerned.
One gets the impression that Bell thinks of her mind as too
wayward and fantastical to have contained any significant
political thought. This serious underestimation of her stat-
ure as a political thinker has lead many people to challenge
Bell's biography. It has blinded people to the consistent
strand of social criticism in her novels and ignores the lu-
cidity and determination with which she brought certain
features of society into focus. An alternative view of her life
would emphasize her lifelong engagement with issues of
public policy, in particular her criticisms of patriarchy and
her defence of pacifism.

Perhaps Bell's fiercest critic has been Jane Marcus, who
writes from a socialist feminist point of view. In articles such
as 'Tintinnabulations', 'Storming the Toolshed' and 'Quentin's Bogey' (in *Art and Anger*, 1988) she criticizes not only
Bell but also many other biographical and psychobiographical studies. She insists on the centrality of political thought
in Virginia Woolf's work. Therefore, she dismisses those
psychobiographers (Poole and Love) who see all of her work
only in terms of her personal obsessions, and are blind to its
public, moral and political content. As for Bell, Marcus claims
that he does not treat Woolf as an intellectual and a writer
but only as a figure of damaged womanhood. His work is
spoiled by his disapproval of Woolf's style of womanhood and
by his belittling of her lifetime's political enagement. She

wishes to replace Bell's view of Woolf as a 'frigid snob, invalid lady, or mad witch' with an image of her as 'the great flaming goddess' (Woolf's phrase) of modern socialist feminism. In Marcus' view Woolf was a revolutionary, a Marxist and a radical mystic (in which she took after her aunt Caroline Emilia Stephen, another important woman writer and thinker ignored or belittled by male historians). Marcus finds evidence of a Marxist aesthetic and a Marxist definition of history in *Moments of Being*. In this claim she has failed to win many supporters. It is worth reading Bell's astonished response (1983) to the idea that Virginia Woolf was a Marxist. There is a judicious arbitration, by Joanne Trautmann (1983), of the battle between Bell (and other members of the Woolf/Bell circle) and the feminist and psychobiographical critics. Bell's book is also criticized by Phyllis Rose (1985) in the context of a general discussion of problems of biography.

More recent biographies have recognized and attempted to understand the central place, the profound existential significance, of writing in Virginia Woolf's life. In Lyndall Gordon's *Virginia Woolf: A Writer's Life*, the story of her life is the story of her creation and re-creation of herself as a writer. Every other aspect of her life is described and analysed from this perspective. Moreover, and in contrast to Bell, Gordon takes it that this central project and narrative is recorded by Woolf in her fiction so that her novels are seen as providing important biographical evidence. Equally, her life story provides us with the essential parameters for reading her fiction. Gordon's book is the most thorough of the full-scale biographical studies to have been written since the full range of Woolf's private papers have been available. Far more than Bell, she has attempted to imagine what it must have been like to be Virginia Woolf, to reconstruct the pattern of her concerns, her memories, values, obsessions and projects, from the inside. She thereby arrives at an account of the well-known facts of her life, her derangement, her traumatized sexuality, her suicide, above all her writing, that identifies their subjective meanings.

The results will not please everybody. Each author highlights different aspects of the story (the sexual abuse, the feminism, the mysticism, the modernism, the relationship to the literary tradition, and so on). In Gordon's view of Woolf's inner world, its dominant feature is that of bereavement. Woolf was haunted by her family ghosts, especially those of her parents, and these ghosts are often transformed into material for her fictions. The important impetus for her writing was the recovery of lost time. Gordon never loses sight of the question of why Woolf wrote, of how writing should be viewed in the context of her inner life. Her interpretation of Woolf's career is unusual. She plays down the importance of her feminism, arguing that Woolf aimed not at rejecting but at redrawing the Victorian model of femininity. Moreover, she argues that it was only for a relatively short part of her career that Woolf can be considered to have been the high priestess of modernism. Since either feminism or modernism or both are most commonly taken to be the central definitions of her fiction, this is clearly a contentious thesis. The emphasis, according to Gordon, is to be placed elsewhere, on Woolf's writing as a search for the unknown. Woolf is seen primarily as a visionary or even as a metaphysical writer, who aimed in her writing to articulate truths about time and reality in the most general sense.

In this light, Gordon says, we should see the decisive moments of Woolf's life story as those which she herself interpreted as moments of revelation, moments in which she felt herself most in touch with reality in some way. These most abstract 'moments of being' are private and non-verbalized experiences and are consequently moments to which the biographer is least likely to have access. Woolf was herself sceptical about the possibility of writing biography precisely because she thought that the most important experiences in a life are not likely to be open to the biographer's view. It is only the fact that she recorded some such moments in her own life in her now published diaries and other papers that enables the biographer to sketch in the main shape of her life, to see the main outlines of her life story. It is this that enables the biographer to deflect attention away from all the scandal, gossip and groundless speculation with which Woolf's life has become encrusted. It is also this definition of the biographer's task that legitimates using the fiction as evidence, because such revelatory moments are most fully depicted in the lives of her fictional characters. For example, consider the famous vision of a fin in a waste of waters, which is attributed to Bernard in *The Waves* but which we know from the diary to have had crucial autobiographical significance for Woolf herself. Gordon's account of Woolf's life refuses to reduce her moments of intensity to purely private, psychobiographical significance, but she also refuses to attribute to politics, in whatever definition, a central and determining role in Woolf's life as a writer. In these ways her account is clearly distinguished from both those of the psychobiographers and those of the feminists.

A different emphasis is provided in Mepham's *Virginia Woolf: A Literary Life*, for although, as the title suggests, it is again Woolf's life as a writer that is given central place in her life story, the interpretation of what writing meant to her, its significance in her lifelong struggle to create and sustain an integrated personality, is more inclusive. Mepham describes the facts of her career as an author: her relations with young, modern writers, the culture of small press publication in which they launched their careers, and above all the Hogarth Press which protected Woolf from interference by editors and publishers and allowed her the freedom to experiment. The most remarkable fact about her writings is that every single one of her books, both fiction and non-fiction, represents a significant difference of technique, an innovation in form. She never settled on any one way of writing, one narrative method, but constantly experimented with new devices, new techniques. Each discovery was adopted, researched and abandoned. Each of these experiments is analysed as a choice, an attempt to find some new way of representing consciousness and life story. Each choice is a way of making a statement about life, about the way the world is, about what it is to be a person, so we can see her career as an endless series of attempts to define what life is, none of them definitive. Her work is a lifelong inconclusive interrogation.

Her constant innovations in form mean that her fictional

worlds are illuminated from different angles, so that different aspects of life and of her own personality are highlighted.
Instead of selecting some single central motivation as the
driving force behind her career, Mepham emphasizes precisely the extent to which she was driven by different, competing motivations, or different aspects of her personality,
and different, contradictory beliefs, between which she made
no final choice. She was attracted alternately to depicting the
inner worlds of her characters and to charting the external,
social and cultural forces which fixed them in their positions.
She was always at war with herself, torn between her different aims. Uncertainty, constant unsettled movement, is the
one central truth of her life around which all her fiction
circulates. The polarities that define her uncertainty have
many names – visionary and materialist, mystic and political, poet and social critic, fact and fantasy, Being and Non-
Being.

The story of Woolf's life as a writer does not, in this
perspective, unduly highlight the great trio of novels from
her most modernist period, *Mrs Dalloway*, *To the Lighthouse*
and *The Waves*. Often the books she wrote before and after
these novels are treated as immature precursors and termi-
nal failures, but Mepham's version of her life story equally
celebrates *Jacob's Room*, *The Years*, *Between the Acts*, her
Diary and 'A Sketch of the Past'. This latter is interpreted as
a profound critique of orthodox forms of life-writing. It is
argued that we should value these works as highly as the
more famous visionary novels, for in them, as in *A Room of
One's Own*, Woolf permits herself to be an angry, disturbing,
even dangerous writer, and these are aspects of herself that
are veiled in the more seductively poetic novels.

Other works of some biographical, but not much literary,
interest are Spater and Parsons (1977), a gossipy and uncritical account of her marriage, and Richard Kennedy's (1978)
slight but entertaining account of his time as a junior em-
ployee at the Hogarth Press. There is some disagreement
about her relationships with her parents: on her father see
Noel Annan (1986); and for the difference of opinion on the
question of Leslie Stephen's support and encouragement of

his daughter, see Katherine Hill and her critics (1981, 1982). Martine Stemerick (1983) and Evelyn Haller (1983) discuss Woolf's relation with her mother. John Lehmann (1975) provides many photographs and Joan Russell Noble (1975) many recollections of Woolf by famous friends and acquaintances. Nigel Nicolson's *Portrait of a Marriage* is useful for her relationship with Vita Sackville-West. Jane Dunn's *A Very Close Conspiracy* is a fine book telling the story of Woolf's relationship with her sister Vanessa Bell. Other relevant sources are mentioned in the section on the Bloomsbury Group in ch. 2.

Psycho-literary Speculations

In 1928 Virginia Woolf wrote an Introduction to an American edition of *Mrs Dalloway*. This was the only time that she gave an account in print of how she had changed the basic plan of one of her novels while writing it, and speculated about the roots of her work in her earliest infantile experiences. It is often referred to by her psychobiographers, for it seems to confirm the idea that elements in her novels can throw light on her early life and on the unconscious, repressed material that underlies her career as a writer. Furthermore, it suggests that the converse is also true, that the biographical and autobiographical record can provide clues for literary interpretation. Some psychobiographers aim primarily to reconstruct the writer's early psychic life, using her fiction as evidence (Jean Love is an example). Others work the other way round and aim mainly at understanding the writer's literary career and her fictional works, using her early life to throw light on her works and her intentions as a writer (Rose is an example of this approach). Poole, Spilka and DeSalvo are somewhere in the middle of the spectrum and in their works the gains in understanding seem to accumulate in both directions. Never have literary criticism and psychobiographic investigation been so intimately entwined as in the case of Virginia Woolf. It is, however, a form of research which is open to the abuse of ungoverned speculation and wild interpretation. It is notable that the various writers in this field have arrived at completely different and incompatible accounts of Woolf's writing, her mental ill health and her suicide.

Perhaps the most influential of psycho-literary studies has been Roger Poole's *The Unknown Virginia Woolf*, originally published in 1978 and reissued in 1982 with a new Preface, which announced a significant modification in his position. Poole's theoretical framework was phenomenological or existential analysis, reminiscent of the work of R.D. Laing and drawing on the philosophical writings of Husserl and Merleau-Ponty. His proposal is that literary studies should aim to draw on both fiction and non-fiction in an attempt 'to reconstruct the subjectivity of the author and its vicissitudes'. The main proposition is that what a person says and does, however bizarre it may seem to others, can be shown to have sense within the subjective experience and existential projects of the person herself. In order to understand that person, therefore, we need to reconstruct the inner life, the meanings and intentions, as the context within which the subject's particular acts can be understood. In Woolf's case Poole takes both her fiction and her non-fiction as providing useful material in this attempt. He also draws upon a reading of Leonard Woolf's novel *The Wise Virgins*, and this was an innovation. His account of Woolf's existential struggles centres on a kind of willed disembodiment, which he sees at work in her anorexia, her refusal of heterosexuality and her suicide, as well as being evident throughout her fiction. His main, and most contested assertion is that it is a damaging mistake to describe her as 'mad'. This labelling, which was perpetrated by her family and her doctors, and which is continued uncritically by Quentin Bell, in Poole's view encouraged people to avoid listening to and trying to understand what she was attempting to say. It legitimated treating her as an object, so that when she raved her husband had her incarcerated, isolated and force-fed, all of which was the exact opposite of what she needed.

This introduces the second feature of Poole's book which has been most heatedly contested – his overwhelmingly negative judgement of Leonard Woolf, who is perceived as an insensitive rationalist whose uncomprehending exercise of power over his wife drove her to rage and despair and eventually to kill herself. This view clashes with the usual view of Leonard's contribution to the marriage as a supportive and untiringly protective husband who, usually successfully, reined in his wife's tendency to extravagant and dangerous excesses of fantasy and anxiety. Poole's account includes a detailed, but not (to me) persuasive, reading of her suicide notes. His book was written as a challenge not just to the orthodoxies of Woolf scholarship but also to those of 'objective' psychiatry. In his 1982 Preface Poole seems to concede that one can use the word 'mad', in general as well as of Virginia Woolf, in a sympathetic rather than a punitive sense. His thesis, in any case, rested on the strange idea that because behaviour could be perceived as subjectively intelligible, it was therefore wrong to consider it insane. There seems little doubt that Virginia Woolf did, at various times in her life, experience a destructive and terrifying loss of control of her mind, that she was, as a result, incapacitated in certain respects, and that she found these experiences so painful that, when threatened by a recurrence in 1941, she chose to kill herself. It is more important to explore the connections, if any, between these facts of her psychic life and her fictions, than to quibble over labels.

The main question from the point of view of literary studies is whether this kind of approach does clarify, or offer interesting and plausible new interpretations of, the author's works. Does reading Woolf's novels as her rendering of her conditions of mental distress and her understanding as to its causes and effects, contribute anything to our understanding of her novels? I would say that there are definite gains in relation to the reading of some fictional characters and episodes, from this way of reading. Perhaps this is so particularly in relation to *The Voyage Out*, which centres on a female character's painful and eventually fatal perplexities concerning her sexuality, to *Night and Day*, which focuses on women's autonomy and creativity and the question of whether they are threatened by marriage, and to the

depiction in *Mrs Dalloway* of the character of Septimus
Warren Smith, one of the few convincing attempts in English
fiction to represent insanity.

A particularly valuable aspect of Poole's position is that he
insists, in contrast to many academic commentators on
Woolf, that her novels cannot be used as evidence that she
achieved a resolution of the conflicting parts of herself. For
example, it is commonly argued that Woolf's concept of the
androgynous mind is a metaphor for her achievement of some
state of harmonious resolution between opposites (masculine
and feminine, and all that they can be taken as standing for).
Poole's position is that embodiment throws us brutally and
irrevocably into a fractured condition, and that it is a
strength of Woolf's novels that they depict life as an inevitable and interminable war between opposites. The assertion
of resolution is no more than wish-fulfilment.

The historical background to the arguments concerning
Woolf's mental condition is documented in Stephen Trombley's *All that Summer she was Mad*, of which the title is a
quotation from Quentin Bell. Trombley's book adopts the
same basic conceptual framework as Poole's. Trombley's idea,
and it turns out to be a very fruitful one, was to go back to
the writings of all the doctors who had a hand in the diagnosis
and treatment of Virginia Woolf and to examine their ideas
about sanity and insanity. These ideas were, from our point
of view, extraordinary and shocking. It is chilling to think of
Woolf in the hands of these men. Her tirade against the
doctor Sir William Bradshaw in *Mrs Dalloway* comes into
sharper focus after reading this book. However, Trombley's
assumption that Woolf cannot properly be called mad, and
his anger with those such as Leonard Woolf and Bell who
have so called her, are not persuasive. He believes that if the
sources of a person's condition and behaviour can be traced
and identified, then she cannot truly be mad. This belief, and
much else in Trombley's book, is criticized by Yeazell (1982).

Jean Love's book, *Virginia Woolf: Sources of Madness and
Art*, was another contribution to psycho-literary studies of
Woolf, but it is weighted heavily towards the psychological
rather than the literary end of the spectrum. Love aimed to

reconstruct in great detail Woolf's early family life and psychic development in an effort to understand her atypical sexuality, her madness and her preoccupation with death. She drew not only on Woolf's private papers, unpublished at that time but now familiar, but also on sources to which few other scholars have referred, notably her parents' letters and other papers. In contrast to other scholars she plays down the influence on Woolf of the sexual abuse she received at the hands of her half-brothers, even considering very seriously the possibility that Woolf may have fantasized it. The precise facts of the matter will never be known and there is a wide range of speculation on the topic. Only towards the end of her book does Love arrive at questions directly connected with literature. She presents a thesis about the relationship between Woolf's madness and her art, a thesis which claims to have some general interest in relation to questions about the psychic sources of artistic work. For her, Woolf's writing was an effort at integration, an attempt to hold together contradictory aspects of her personality. Lack of order in her experience was the common ground of both her madness and her art. Her unusual, almost hallucinatory, capacity for imaginative creation of fictional scenes provided her with the possibility of controlling material which otherwise threatened her mental stability.

Mark Spilka's *Virginia Woolf's Quarrel with Grieving* is an excellent example of what he calls 'psycho-literary speculations'. More modest in its scope than the books by Poole and Love, this study concentrates on the long repressed knot of entangled emotional reactions to her parents' deaths, reactions which were not finally excavated and resolved until Woolf was near the end of her life. Throughout her career she returned again and again in her fiction to the representation of bereavement, from that of Rachel Vinrace in *The Voyage Out* to that of Delia Pargiter in *The Years*. Spilka's argument is that Woolf's anxiety and emotional confusion are betrayed in her uncertain handling of this theme. The choices she makes in her fiction register the unfinished business of mourning that burdened her own life. Her inability to disentangle and resolve her repressed emotional reactions of

anger, guilt and grief, particularly in response to her
mother's death, not only contributed to her lack of mental
balance but also led her to make choices in her fiction which
leave the reader puzzled and dissatisfied.

An example is her decision to split the main character in
Mrs Dalloway into two, so that Septimus, who shares Woolf's
incapacitating inability to grieve, is burdened with insanity
and eventually suicide, while his double, Clarissa Dalloway,
is left free to pursue her life. Spilka also provides a close
analysis of Lily Briscoe's delayed grief in *To the Lighthouse*.
What is missing in this novel is any account of the history of
Lily's sexuality. What is it that has produced her terror of
physical love? Her lack of psychic history is connected to
Woolf's inability to understand her own. Spilka's other detailed analysis is of Delia Pargiter's reactions to her mother's
death in *The Years*. His was among the first detailed analyses
of 'A Sketch of the Past', the main non-fictional source for
most authors' speculations on these topics. What is distinctive about his approach is that it starts from a sense of
dissatisfaction with the novels, which he tries to trace to its
source, rather than being based on the assumption that the
novels successfully represent a resolution of their characters'
emotional confusions. We are reminded that literary texts
are not immaculately conceived in some zone of disembodied

artistic inspiration but are the hard-won results of their
authors' struggles to find clarifying fictional equivalents to
their painful psychic realities. It is this way of thinking about
literature that ultimately justifies the speculative attempts
to make connections between authors' psychobiographies
and the fictional worlds which they create.

Another virtue of Spilka's way of pursuing these enquiries
is that his broad view includes not only questions about
Virginia Woolf's own oddities of personality but also the
general cultural and historical problems relating to responses to death. Woolf's confrontation of the brutality and
senselessness of the deaths in her family reflects a general
cultural trend, the loss of cultural resources of ritual and
ceremony for dealing with our private disasters. Virginia
Woolf's traumas were not the result merely of an over-

sensitive woman's weakness, but had broad cultural significance. This is the theme also of Mepham's 'Mourning and
Modernism' which shows how Woolf's experiments with literary form in her novels can be seen as an attempt to find an
adequate language of mourning in specific historical conditions. Her belief that death, whether in the family or in the
First World War, is a senseless disaster with no compensation
or consolatory meanings, is connected with her rejection of
the literary forms of character and life story in her novels.

Spilka (1979) surveys the psychobiographical work that
flourished in the late 1970s, and this article is a useful
overview and comparison of the results of the work of Spilka
himself, Poole, Love and Rose (whose book I discuss later
under a different heading). He expresses some scepticism
concerning Love's theory of the sources of art and argues
against Poole's eccentric views about the Woolfs' marriage
and his anachronistic views about her 'madness'. Gindin
(1981) also discusses and criticizes the books of Poole, Rose
and Love.

More recent psychobiographical studies have demonstrated not only the rewards, but also the extreme dangers
of this kind of work. Louise DeSalvo (1989) sees sexual abuse
both as the single most important formative factor in Woolf's
life and as having had a decisive influence on her work. Her
book provides a very detailed picture of family life in the
Stephen household, emphasizing the violence of feeling and
the extreme sexual tension that permeated the family. In
DeSalvo's account, every member of this large family was
involved either as perpetrator or as victim in violent inces-
tuous sexual abuse. Going far beyond what previous authors
have claimed, she asserts that Woolf was abused continuously over many years. Her account of Woolf's psychological
development plays down the factor that other writers have
seen as crucial, the successive severe traumas caused by the
deaths of so many members of her family. However, there is
a serious problem with the style of argument in this book.
Speculations about sexual abuse, which are impossible to
substantiate on the known evidence, are presented as established facts. What evidence there is is subjected to one-sided

interpretation. No effort is made to test alternative hypotheses, to examine other plausible views either about the facts of the matter or about the general narrative of Woolf's development. The style of argument is more like partisan legal advocacy than balanced scholarly judgement.

Some of the crucial steps in DeSalvo's account depend on her reading of Woolf's juvenilia; for example, the story 'A Cockney's Farming Experience', written when she was ten and another, 'A Terrible Tragedy in a Duckpond', dating from 1899 when she was seventeen. These stories, normally read as lighthearted and witty diversions, are taken by DeSalvo to be coded narratives of child sexual abuse. Fortunately, the latter story, according to DeSalvo an imaginary suicide and a desperate cry for help, has subsequently been published so the reader can now make up his or her own mind. DeSalvo's claims are subjected to a detailed but good-humoured scrutiny by Quentin Bell (1990), who was the first to call attention to the evidence for abuse but who insists on the thinness of that evidence, which prevents us from knowing the precise nature, frequency or degree of abuse to which the young Virginia Stephen was subjected.

Perhaps one gain from this line of work as far as literary studies are concerned is that it can turn attention to aspects of Woolf's novels that are otherwise relatively neglected. For example, DeSalvo looks closely at Woolf's representation of children in her novels. Childhood experience is, she says, presented as unremittingly bleak and terrifying. Her view is that the novels portray children as ignored, betrayed, abandoned or abused. This approach does throw light from an unexpected angle on some of the novels. For example, *Jacob's Room* is, from this perspective, a novel about single-parenting and its effects.

The dangers of psychobiography are illustrated by Alma Halbert Bond's *Who Killed Virginia Woolf? A Psychobiography* which, as the title suggests, reviews the main relationships in Woolf's life and asks which of them contributed towards her suicide. The book is another attack on what is seen as a family conspiracy to prevent the truth of Woolf's life from being told, in an effort to preserve reputations.

Leonard Woolf and Vanessa Bell come in for severe rebuke. Woolf's life is seen as a series of betrayals. The most important accusations are speculations for which no evidence is presented and the uncontrolled narrative invention on which so much psychobiography is based results in the postulation of utterly different and quite incompatible stories. For example, Bond argues that sexual abuse, the central drama of Virginia Stephen's childhood according to DeSalvo, was of no consequence whatsoever and may not have taken place at all. This illustrates the extreme care with which the results of this kind of work must be approached.

Critical Reception to 1965

The history of reactions to Woolf's work can be followed in Majumdar and McLaurin (1975), an extremely useful anthology of essays and reviews. It begins with the reviews of *The Voyage Out* in 1915 and goes through to the obituaries on her death in 1941. The volume collects 135 items and has, in addition, a good introduction which summarizes the history of her reception and the kinds of issues which her critics discussed. This, together with Kirkpatrick's bibliography (1980), are indispensible aids to any research on Woolf's career.

An essay by Forster written in 1926 tells us that the initial response to Woolf's novels in the 1920s was to see her as a talented writer in an impressionistic mode, who could produce prose of dazzling but baffling beauty. Doubts remained, however, about her ability to depict external realities. The reviews collected in this anthology confirm that she was regarded as unconventional, as avant-garde, as belonging to a group of modern, experimental, 'stream of consciousness' writers, along with Joyce, Dorothy Richardson and Katherine Mansfield. This view was encouraged by her own essays in which she attempted to articulate her aims as a writer, and especially by 'Modern Novels' (written in 1919 and revised as 'Modern Fiction' in 1925). It is here that one finds those phrases that are almost universally quoted in

critics' discussions of her fiction, the 'luminous halo' and
'semi-transparent envelope', the 'myriad impressions' and
the 'shower of atoms' falling on the mind, and so on. She
returned to the task of defining the aims of the modern
writers in a series of essays written in 1923-5 ('Mr Bennett
and Mrs Brown' and 'Character in Fiction'). The different
versions of these can be read in *The Essays of Virginia Woolf*
vol. 3. Her argument with Arnold Bennett and the significance of these essays are discussed in Hynes (1972), Daugherty (1983) and Mepham (1991).

Clive Bell was an early champion of his sister-in-law's
work, as we can see in his 1924 essay. E.M. Forster's assessment in 1926 is very positive, though he still harbours some
doubts on the question of character. Woolf's growing reputation, from *To the Lighthouse* in 1927 onwards, can be traced
in the increasingly respectful discussions of her work by such
as Eliot (1927), Storm Jameson (1928) and Empson (1931).
The latter, in particular, raised interesting questions about
the nature of Woolf's modernism. By the end of the 1930s her
work had at last reached a wide readership, especially
through *Orlando* and *The Years*, and she was also becoming
well known in France and Japan. There were, however,
attacks on her work. Majumdar and McLaurin reprint a
famously negative review of *Three Guineas* by Queenie
Leavis, whose husband wrote a brutally dismissive review of
Between the Acts in 1941. Overviews of her career, written at
the time of her death and reprinted here, include pieces by
Edwin Muir, Stephen Spender and E.M. Forster.

The earliest book in English on Virginia Woolf was Winifrid Holtby's *Virginia Woolf: A Critical Memoir*, published in
1932. Written while Woolf was still in mid-career, this study
is clearly incomplete, but it is nonetheless a fine book.
Holtby's chapter on *Jacob's Room* remains one of the most
perceptive responses to that difficult novel ever written. She
compares the construction of the novel with 'cinematograph
technique', seeing the transitionless discontinuity of narrative as analogous to film montage. By and large, however,
the quality of book-length studies on Woolf's fiction in the 20
years after her death was not outstanding and few books

from those years have much interest today. They are surveyed in Jean Guiguet's magisterial study of 1965. Guiguet's was the first major study to become established as the central reference work on the subject and to survive as such for many years. It is discussed in ch. 5. Of the books on Woolf from this period perhaps it is worth mentioning David Daiches (1963). He concentrates on the delicacy of her rendering of experience and the mood of twilight reverie in her novels. This is rather a restricted view of her achievements. Daiches' book was originally published in 1942, very shortly after Woolf's death, at which time he believed her to be a minor writer. Later he modified this opinion. Daiches' *The Novel and the Modern World* contains a shorter version of his views on Woolf.

Bibliographies and Reference Works

B.J. Kirkpatrick's meticulous *Bibliography of Virginia Woolf* lists and describes all of Woolf's publications, including all of her essays, reviews, pamphlets and so on, as known at the time of the 3rd edition in 1980, in all of their many editions, and gives very detailed information about print runs, sales and translations. Such is the volume of information available about the details of Woolf's life in her papers and those of her husband that Edward Bishop (1989), in his chronology, is able to provide an account of her activities almost on a day-by-day basis. The 220 pages of chronology list the details of her social life, her travels, her journalism, her work for the Hogarth Press, her friendships, family life, marriage and illnesses.

There are two books that document Woolf's literary sources and allusions. Elizabeth Steele (1983) provides a guide to those of her essays which are in the *Collected Essays* volumes. There is an index and this makes it possible to find all references to any particular author. This information is now being absorbed into the more comprehensive *Essays of Virginia Woolf*. Beverly Ann Schlack (1979) lists allusions in five of Woolf's novels. The fact that there turns out to be such a large number of them draws attention to allusion as an important feature of her style. Schlack analyses the significance of allusion, its contribution to Woolf's methods of characterization, theme and structure. The quite extraordinary wealth of allusion, to myth as well as to literary sources, and consequently the density of meaning that Woolf achieves, are shown with very useful results.

This serves as a reminder that Virginia Woolf was a formidable reader. Brenda Silver's *Virginia Woolf's Reading Notebooks* lists the contents of some thirty notebooks and many papers in which Woolf recorded her reading and made notes for her journalism, and for both her fiction and non-fiction books.

There have been several bibliographies of the secondary literature on Woolf. In a special issue of *Modern Fiction Studies* (of which, incidentally, the colophon is a lighthouse!) in 1972, Barbara Weiser provided a checklist of criticism from 1956-72. Robin Majumdar (1976) brings the list a little more up-to-date and provides some useful annotations. The most recent, and by far the most thorough, of bibliographies of secondary works is that of Thomas Rice (1984) which includes foreign works and a checklist of dissertations. Rice lists a daunting 1358 items (up to the end of 1983, and the flood has not diminished since then) and provides very useful evaluative annotations and four indexes, all of which adds up to an impressive guide for those who wish to conduct research in this field.

2

Virginia Woolf and her Context

'The Real World'

In England, until recently, most discussion of Virginia Woolf's work focused on one of two topics. Either she was seen as a narrow writer, restricted to exploring the subtleties of subjective experience, or the main interest in her was centred on her psychological history and the way in which her obsessions and traumas found expression in her fiction. Of course, there were some exceptions to these dominant tendencies, and in the USA in the 1980s feminists began to open up an important new perspective on her work. By and large, though, the consensus view was that Woolf was not interested in the external world. She did not aim either to depict or, through her writing, to reform, the world of social and political relations and institutions. Forster (1942) had said that 'improving the world she would not consider' and Jean Guiguet (1965) said in his very influential book that 'the mechanical relations between individuals, such as are imposed by the social structure, dominated by concepts of class and wealth...are not her problem.' The Marxist critic Arnold Kettle was of the view that Woolf promoted 'the development of a cult of sensibility, inadequately based on the realities of the social situation'. These propositions were quoted by Alex Zwerdling (1986) in his immensely refreshing and provocative book, *Virginia Woolf and the Real World,* in which he challenged the view that Woolf's work was apolitical and that

25

personal thought - consciousness is the most important part of life anyway so why should its depiction be seen as limited?

she was indifferent to social issues. In this book, a quite different Virginia Woolf comes into focus. He argues that she was fascinated by social power and its mechanisms all her life, was driven by the desire to challenge and change power relations in society and was a social critic and reformer, not just in her feminist pamphlets, but throughout her fiction. The perception of her as exclusively interested in the stream of subjective life is one-sided and blinds us to some of the great riches of her novels, for she was aware that our private experience is shaped by social institutions and sought to depict the processes of this formation. Her work has, from beginning to end, epic and satirical dimensions hardly glimpsed in orthodox criticism.

Of course, some feminist writers had already reminded us that Woolf was a lifelong critic of patriarchy and it would be wrong to credit Zwerdling with total originality on these issues. He agrees with Rose (1978) that feminism was the crux of her emotional and intellectual life. Nevertheless, some American feminist studies of Woolf make serious errors of judgement, he claims. Criticising Marcus (1981, 1983) he argues that there is a tendency to exaggerate or to oversimplify her social criticism and to credit her with ideas in an ahistorical way. The views that are attributed to her by Marcus, in fact reflect the latter's own cultural and political preoccupations and not the specific historical experience of women of Woolf's class and generation. Therefore, they miss many of the ambiguities, the hesitations and contradictions of her thinking. Marcus was right, though, to point out that feminism did not exhaust Woolf's ideas on society, for she was concerned with a wider range of issues than patriarchy and gender. Her thoughts, especially about class and wealth, pushed her in other directions. In any case, Zwerdling claims, her views collapsed under the pressure of historical events from the end of the 1930s, and it is very important to study her works each in its specific period and not to assume that her thinking achieved an unchanging lifelong coherence.

Zwerdling's book contains two kinds of material: detailed analysis of the social content of her works, and studies of the specific historical context in which they were written and without which we miss much of their meaning. Moreover, he shows that there is a connection between her experimental narrative techniques and her purposes as a social critic. For example, there has been much comment in relation to the problem of character in *Jacob's Room*. We never get to know Jacob Flanders, for he is not constructed as a rounded character on the usual novelistic model. Most comment on this fact has concentrated on the general epistemological issues involved; we can never get to know other people, what motivates them remains always a mystery to us, and so on. But the reason why Jacob remains unknown to the narrator is more specific and more historical; it is because he died as a young man before his identity had had a chance to form, and because he died as a soldier in the First World War. *Jacob's Room* is an anti-war novel and it is full of specific and biting social comment on the mechanisms of cultural conditioning that turn young men into the willing victims of militaristic ideology. The novel discloses the connections between the ancient universities, with their apparent dedication to learning, and the class system that reproduces in each generation the arrogant inheritors of power and privilege. Jacob is simultaneously loved, as a confused and shy young man, and feared and resented because of the roles that he is destined to play in public life. This is a theme that is also the subject of Sara Ruddick's excellent article (1981).

Zwerdling discusses *Mrs Dalloway* as an examination of the governing class of England in 1923, enfeebled by its failure to absorb the lessons of the First World War. He examines the detailed historical texture of the novel and its depiction of the specific circumstances: the stupidity of the ruling class, the prevalence of patriotism, patriarchal bullying and worship of royalty and empire. These circumstances drove some victims to misery and suicide, while others settled for safety and comfort and abandoned their youthful thirst for rapturous experience.

In his chapter on *To the Lighthouse* Zwerdling investigates the Victorian family and its rapid disappearance at the turn of the century, and Woolf's scepticism at the new liberation plot, which modern writers saw as representing salvation, as

The family's sense of loss and grief. *Virginia Woolf*

attainable by emancipation from family ties. Other topics include the withering, in the 1930s, of Bloomsbury optimism about the progressive power of the elite of civilizing individuals, and Woolf's disillusionment, towards the end of her life, when the optimism that had sustained her pacifism, collapsed through her reading of Freud and the threat of fascism. Zwerdling gives a detailed picture of the culture of 1930s pacifism. It is a pity that he does not examine in detail the arguments of *Three Guineas*, Woolf's most contentious and exasperating book. Zwerdling is stronger on contextual detail than on textual analysis.

Among his most valuable contributions is his examination of Woolf's attitudes to class and wealth. The context was the anti-egalitarian and undemocratic elitism of Bloomsbury, expressed most unattractively in Clive Bell's *Civilisation*. Virginia Woolf and some of her friends assumed that the elite families, constituting a wealthy and leisured class, performed a necessary social role of providing an intellectual aristocracy. This group was taken to be entrusted with the function of embodying and carrying forward all the virtues of civilization. These virtues were thought of as sensitivity to aesthetic form and the cultivation of delightful and intellectually rewarding friendships. Between the wars these assumptions came under attack, and Woolf and her friends had an anxious, uncertain view of their social role. Threatened by the aggressiveness of the working class and the philistinism of the middle class, their snobbery and cultural arrogance were vulnerable to guilt, panic and despair. Woolf's own class feelings were increasingly uneasy and the portrait of the artist in an inattentive and ungrateful English society in *Between the Acts*, shows how far she had drifted into pessimism by the end of her life.

 One particular historical episode to which Woolf's reactions were very revealing, but which is scarcely mentioned by Zwerdling, was the General Strike of 1926. Kate Flint (1986) pulls together all the evidence as to Woolf's reactions to it, including her differences on the issue with her husband, who strongly supported the striking miners. Although Woolf joined in the political activity, her interest was very limited.

Her mind was sometimes on more abstract, less political, things – the strike coincided with her composition of the 'Time Passes' section of *To the Lighthouse*. During the strike she also went clothes shopping with the editor of *Vogue* magazine, to buy a fur coat. Moreover, the strike brought out her nervousness about the working class and her perception of them as violent and uncivilized, a force for social disintegration. Flint notes the evidence of these ways of thinking not only in Woolf's diary but also in her novels.

Marxist Views

American radical feminist interpretations of Woolf are at their weakest, in my view, on the questions of her class position and her attitudes to class. Some have been seduced into believing that she was a socialist, or even a marxist, by the fact that she taught briefly at Morley College and belonged to the Labour Party. In this they betray their lack of comprehension both of British Labourism and of that complex and exasperating nightmare, the British class system. As I have noted above, there is much evidence that Woolf's political instincts were far from democratic. Certainly her membership of the Labour Party and the Fabian Society are no evidence to the contrary. As for her class position, there is a subtle analysis of it from a Marxist point of view by Raymond Williams (1980), in the context of his study of the Bloomsbury Group. This Group had a very particular class origin in a segment of the upper-middle-class professional and intellectual elite, based in the ancient universities. They were in a position to grasp, as the main body of the ruling class were not, the desperate need for cultural and institutional modernization. The function of the universities in training the elite cadres for the state and the professions was handicapped by the absurd relics of Victorian culture. In Williams' account, the Bloomsbury Group were a fraction of this social stratum of which the origins, attitudes and ideology were reflected in their predominantly elitist and individualist ways of thinking. They stressed the culturally central role of the 'civilised individual'. The need for this hero (or heroine) of social change, the main agent of social and cultural progress, required the perpetuation of a wealthy leisured class. In other words, they saw themselves as a necessary intellectual aristocracy, rooted in and sustained by unearned income.

There is, unfortunately, very little significant Marxist criticism of Woolf's fiction. What there is has centred on *Mrs Dalloway*. As an example of an American feminist view of the ideology of this novel we might take the remark by Suzette Henke (1981) that '*Mrs Dalloway* offers a scathing indictment of the British class system and a strong critique of patriarchy.' Perhaps it would be fair to say that the weakness of this position is that it oversimplifies Woolf's attitudes to class in the novel, whereas the weakness of the Marxist interpretations is that they have shown little interest in her critique of patriarchy. The analysis of her class attitudes was initiated by William Empson in an article originally published in 1932 (and reprinted in 1987). Empson recognized that Woolf used some of her characters as a way of disowning the snobbish and patriotic sentiments of both her own and other classes. Nonetheless, he argues, Woolf's voice can be heard declaiming that after all such things can be felt with decent honesty. She can see the point of view of the snobs and the patriots. Her position is ambivalent and she sides with both the ruling elite and their critics. For example, in *Mrs Dalloway*, she makes fun of and yet also admires the aristocratic and powerful guests at Clarissa Dalloway's party.

This analysis is extended and developed by Eagleton (1970) who argues that Woolf suffered both an intense, snobbish concern with fashionable, worldly success and at the same time a lucid awareness of the pointlessness of this whole charade. In *Mrs Dalloway*, Peter Walsh is the character through whom she represents a socially critical viewpoint, but she does not simply endorse his views. She encourages the reader to perceive Walsh as a misfit and a crank. In the end, the novel both criticizes and upholds the social conventions of English upper-class life. In this it is typical of what Eagleton calls 'the upper-class novel', in that it reveals the common tension between the unquestioned public values of social hierarchy and tradition and the private values of the contemplative aesthetic or visionary experience (experience of 'timeless intensities, contemplative privacy, "metaphysical" probings', in Eagleton's words). The world in which these latter values flourish is itself part of the former world, the upper-class world of privileged leisure and wealth, and cannot be a point from which to launch unambiguous social criticism of it. Virginia Woolf represents a class stratum which, while deviating from the values of the ruling class, is parasitic upon it and depends upon it for protection against the exigencies of forced work, social responsibility and material hardship. It should be no surprise, therefore, if Woolf and her circle cannot form an alliance with those who would attack the class system frontally, in the name of social equality. In short, Woolf's values, as expressed in her novels, are simultaneously deviations from and reflections of upper-class life. There is a mass of evidence for her ignorance of the world of physical labour and for her inability to imagine the lives it leads to, in her novels, her diary and her essay 'Memories of a Working Women's Guild'. The other side to this is her tendency always to aesthetisise experience in her novels as if no experience could be significant for her unless, as in one of her 'moments of being', it could be conceived as opening up a vision of ultimate reality. It is as if she had no inkling of physical work and its satisfaction. As David Lodge (no Marxist) pointed out (1977): 'We do not always think of eternity while serving potatoes: sometimes we just think of serving potatoes. Virginia Woolf's characters never do.'

The most extended analysis of *Mrs Dalloway*, in fact, the only book-length Marxist study of Woolf's work, is Hawthorn's *Virginia Woolf's* Mrs Dalloway: *A Study in Alienation*. His interpretation starts from what he sees as Clarissa Dalloway's split personality and Septimus Warren Smith's madness. Both of these he sees, in characteristic Marxist fashion, as not just individual pathologies but as having their roots in the social system. He argues that Woolf had only a partial view of the material world of work and social relations. In *Mrs Dalloway* she demonstrates her belief that human community or social synthesis is created not in and through collective work but in a party gathering of the leisured class. She herself lacked the kinds of communal social experience which would have allowed her to portray convincing solutions to Clarissa's problems, her social alienation and her dissatisfaction. Woolf's conception of 'life' (that etherial 'luminous halo'!) was damagingly incomplete.

Woolf and Psychoanalysis

Many authors have pointed out the main facts concerning Virginia Woolf's contact with psychoanalytic ideas. Her brother and sister-in-law, Adrian and Karin Stephen, were psychoanalysts. Members of her Bloomsbury circle translated Freud's works into English and they were published by the Woolfs' Hogarth Press. In spite of these facts, Woolf seems not to have read Freud until 1939. Studying his work at that time caused, or coincided with, an important change in her general ideas about society and culture and entered significantly into the composition of *Between the Acts* (Zwerdling, 1986; Mepham, 1991).

There is now, in Elizabeth Abel's *Virginia Woolf and the Fictions of Psychoanalysis*, a more detailed study of Woolf's relation with the history of psychoanalysis in England and a suggestion that this relation is more complicated than had hitherto been thought. The centre of Abel's argument is the contrast between two different narratives of development, each of which is central in a different, competing psychoanalytic tradition. There is a Freudian narrative of development, in which the Oedipal triangle and the resolution of the Oedipal complex are central to the development of the child's personality. In this narrative the memory of the mother as an object of love is repressed. The passage to maturity is the development of language and of the reality principle, which is the recognition of the gulf that separates the world from our desires. On the other hand, there is the narrative of development as conceived by Melanie Klein, which was important in English analytical circles in the 1920s. In this it is the relation with the mother which is, and remains, crucial. The child enters the symbolic and cultural order not by repressing but by symbolically recreating its prelinguistic experience of the mother. In the Kleinian narrative the mother–infant relation, characterized by uncertain boundaries and aggressive fantasies, is central and can reappear in later creative activity, especially in visual art, in attempts to reconstitute through visual imagination a zone in which subject and object are only partially distinct. Abel provides evidence that there was a battle between these two competing theories, and more generally an argument as to the roles played by the mother and the father in psychic development, not only in psychoanalytic circles but also in literature and anthropology in Britain in the 1920s.

Woolf's acquaintance with and interest in these arguments shows up in her fiction, for the two competing narratives are to be found, according to Abel, in *To the Lighthouse*. James' development is conceived in typically Freudian, Oedipal terms. He achieves an objective grasp of the world and represses the memory of his relationship with his mother. Lily Briscoe, on the other hand, experiences a Kleinian development. In Part I of the novel, although she is an adult, she enjoys or conceives the possibility of an ecstatic fusion with her surrogate mother, Mrs Ramsay. Ten years later, after Mrs Ramsay's death, Lily works at her painting and recovers an image of her 'mother'. The memory of the earliest intimacy with the mother is, in Lily's life as it was in Woolf's own, a haunting image of ecstatic union. The origin of artistic creativity is the attempt to register and recreate such infantile experience within the represented world. In the 1920s Woolf celebrated a maternal origin of culture, both in *To the Lighthouse* and in the idea of thinking back through our mothers in *A Room of One's Own*.

Abel's argument is that Woolf's thinking shifted so that in the 1930s she moved to a Freudian position. In *Three Guineas* her identity is no longer given by her place in the maternal tradition but by her being the daughter of an educated man. There is in *Three Guineas* no positive image of the mother to counterbalance the aggression of the father, and the book's message is rather a bleak one. The shift to a paternal genealogy and the associated pessimism, the lack of any faith in amelioration via the positive creative power of a maternally inspired art, are also to be found in *Between the Acts*. It was in the period when she was writing this book that Woolf for the first time read Freud for herself. She read Freud on war and death, and *Group Psychology and the Analysis of the Ego*, works which pessimistically postulate the permanence of aggression and the limited recuperative powers of art.

The Bloomsbury Group

Woolf's most immediate cultural context, apart from her family, was the Bloomsbury Group, a circle of friends assembled from her brothers' acquaintances at Cambridge University, many of whom became very significant figures in various fields of English intellectual and artistic life. Lytton Strachey was a biographer, Maynard Keynes was an economist, Clive Bell and Roger Fry were art critics and writers on aesthetics, Duncan Grant and Vanessa Bell were painters, Leonard Woolf was a writer on politics and international affairs, and E.M. Forster, a friend of Virginia Woolf who was on the fringes of Bloomsbury, was a novelist. Questions as to the exact membership and nature of the group, its aspirations and values and the extent to which it can be understood by reference to the intellectual trends dominant in Cambridge in the first decade of this century, have all been much discussed. They are important in relation to Virginia Woolf in as much as many people have perceived the beliefs, assumptions and ideals expressed in her writing, as well as its formal, experimental features, to have been heavily influenced by her immersion in Bloomsbury culture, from the formation of the group in 1904 through the rest of her life. Her own wonderfully funny description of 'Old Bloomsbury', i.e., of them in the period when they were still young people just setting up a life for themselves away from family and university, is in *Moments of Being*. An extensive insider's discussion of their beliefs and activities can be found in Leonard Woolf's autobiography. I have mentioned in the previous section Raymond Williams' subtle analysis of the historical significance of the Group. Essays by Holroyd and Annan in Marcus (1987) are also worth looking at.

Perhaps the most readable extensive account of the group is Leon Edel's work (1979). Edel is a literary biographer who, in this book, traces the intertwining lives of the nine central members of the Group from their youth through to the 1920s. There is very little here that deals directly with Virginia Woolf's literary career (indeed her development as a novelist was only beginning in the early 1920s when the book closes), but Edel does provide an introduction to the general social and cultural milieu. Other useful biographical sources are Holroyd (1971) and Frances Spalding's (1983) biography of Virginia's sister Vanessa Bell.

Edel's book closes with a discussion of one of the key documents in Bloomsbury history, Maynard Keynes' 1938 Memoir Club paper, published as 'My Early Beliefs'. In this Keynes looks back 35 years and more to the days when many Bloomsbury men (not the women, of course, for they were denied a university education) were students at Cambridge. He discusses the influence upon them of the thought and writing of the Cambridge philosopher G.E. Moore and argues that those who at the time were hostile to them, notably D.H. Lawrence, had correctly identified something weak and naive in their position, particularly in their values which placed friendship and the contemplation of beauty above all else. In a famous image, he asserted that they had been like water spiders skimming the surface of a pool with no conception at all of the forces and currents beneath. In their attachment to what they thought of as civilization, they were blind to the aggression, violence and irrationality that were to become such appallingly destructive forces in European history at a later date. The extent to which this was a fair assessment of the early Bloomsbury culture and the extent to which they later came to have quite different beliefs and attachments is much debated. Quentin Bell's short book *Bloomsbury* (1968) is an excellent and characteristically

elegant introduction to the debates. He was himself associated with the Group through his family, yet he was nonetheless, as a 1930s Marxist, highly critical of its establishment
status. Even so, he was clearly irritated by the many ignorant
and unfair criticisms to which the Group was subjected in
the days when it still attracted heated reactions and partisan
polemic. This is a view from very close up, an account which
is often anecdotal, but with some valuable clarifications (e.g.,
about relations with Rupert Brooke and D.H. Lawrence). He
throws doubt on the accuracy of Keynes' paper, arguing that
it was a deliberate provocation addressed to the younger
members of the Memoir Club. Bloomsbury is seen by Bell, as
it was in Leonard Woolf's account, not as a Group cemented
together by a common manifesto or programme, but as held
together by mutual affection, and whose one common belief
was in the importance of rational discussion of issues, their
perception that the sleep of reason engenders monsters of
violence.

These questions are important for an understanding of
Virginia Woolf, and they connect particularly with the issue
raised earlier about her reading of Freud, her increasing
pessimism in the 1930s and its effects on *Three Guineas* and
Between the Acts. It is a question of the extent to which, or
the manner in which, she understood the discontents of
civilization. The extent to which Bloomsbury thinkers in
general, and Virginia Woolf in particular, underestimated
'the vulgar passions' is discussed in Quentin Bell (1979).
Keynes' paper, and many of the other main sources for an
understanding of Bloomsbury, are collected together in the
extremely useful volume edited by S.P. Rosenbaum (1975).
This contains a large number of descriptions by Group members themselves of their activities and controversies, as well
as observations and criticisms of the Group by associates as
well as outsiders, both friendly and hostile. Virginia Woolf
figures in the collection both with some of her writings and
as observed by her friends, such as T.S. Eliot and E.M.
Forster.

I do not think it would be unfair to say that most of the
sources I have mentioned so far on the topic of Bloomsbury

are anecdotal or biographical and contribute only superficially to the intellectual history of the Group as a context for the work of Virginia Woolf. A book which is much more substantial in this respect is S.P. Rosenbaum's *Victorian Bloomsbury*. This volume covers only the early background to Bloomsbury thought, particularly the thought of their parents' generation, and the literary and philosophical culture of Cambridge University up to the early years of the present century. On these topics see also Rosenbaum (1983). The question of the influence of that culture on Virginia Woolf, and especially of the influence of G.E. Moore, is a puzzling one. Rosenbaum provides an introduction to Moore's thought which was certainly the dominant influence on those of his students who were to become members of Bloomsbury. He was worshipped by Leonard Woolf. Rosenbaum claims that Moore's philosophy, and not only his ethics but also his refutation of idealism, were influential on Virginia Woolf's work. The case for the importance of Moore's thought, and also that of William James, as influences on Virginia Woolf, is presented by Harvena Richter (1970) who argues that Moore's central contribution was his theory of perception, of the relationship between consciousness and the external world, which was important in the formation of Woolf's way of thinking about subjectivity, the cornerstone to all her work. The case for assessing Moore's influence, and indeed that of any other philosopher apart from Plato, as minimal is presented by Mepham (1991). Poole (1978) argues that Woolf's thinking about experience and language was precisely the opposite of Moore's, for the question with which he always pursued his philosophical conversations, 'What exactly do you mean by that?', was based on a belief in clarity and unequivocal meaning that Woolf, unlike her rationalist husband, rejected. Not only did she reject it but the whole style of her work and thought depended upon that rejection.

Poole also poses the broader question of just how much Virginia Woolf should be seen as having shared the Bloomsbury Group's ways of thinking. It is usually assumed that because she was married to Leonard Woolf and was herself a member of the Group, there must have been a great deal in common in their most fundamental assumptions. But according to Poole it would be more accurate to see her relationship to Bloomsbury as that of an undercover agent in enemy territory. So unsympathetic was she to what they stood for that she was not the Group's priestess but its Antigone. Some other writers have also wanted to play down the importance of the Group and to emphasize instead the influence of usually neglected women, especially her aunts, Caroline Stephen (see Marcus, 1988) and Anny Thackeray (see MacKay, 1987), her friend Violet Dickinson (see Hawkes, 1981) and the anthropologist Jane Harrison (see Shattuck, 1987). Another perspective on Woolf's intellectual parentage is offered by Meisel (1980), who argues for her affiliation to Walter Pater. His book traces the influence of Paterian aesthetics in Woolf's habits of thought, notably in her essays.

Bloomsbury Aesthetics

By far the most important aspect of Bloomsbury thought from the point of view of Virginia Woolf's own work is the writing on art by Clive Bell and Roger Fry. Roger Fry was most famous for his introduction into England of Post-Impressionist painting in two exhibitions, in 1910 and 1912, and for his writings about art, notably *Vision and Design*, *Transformations* and his book on Cézanne. Bell in *Art* (1913) introduced the term 'significant form', to designate what it is about a work of art that gives it value and that appeals to our aesthetic sense. It was argued that this form was to be distinguished from the content or subject matter of art, and most particularly from the narrative and moralistic content of so much Victorian art. For the work of art should be autonomous, which is to say, should create its own meanings or significance independently of meanings or significance which derive from practical or other non-aesthetic realms of experience. But why, in that case, is art supposed to have such a very high value? Does the 'significant form' in some way refer to or represent something transcendental? What does significant form signify? Does art, including writing, have a metaphysical vocation? Certainly both Bell and Woolf did sometimes talk as if this were so. 'Ultimate reality' or the 'underlying reality' are terms in which they try to explain the special virtue of art. Whereas life is confusingly chaotic and shapeless, art, it seems, is an expression of order or pattern, or the discovery of order or pattern. This sort of vocabulary was common to both the painters and the writers in Bloomsbury. Virginia Woolf often spoke of her search for 'unity' and 'pattern'. E.M. Forster, in *Aspects of the Novel* (1927), asserted that art is 'the one orderly product which our muddling race has produced'. What, one wonders, about science, chess, football, religion, government or cooking, or any of the other traditions and institutions which order our experience? Why, for Bloomsbury, and indeed for other modernist artists and writers, was art supposed to be so very superior and important, so much of the essence of civilization? Why, also, was it thought to be so vital to keep it free of politics and 'personality'? Roger Fry, and Woolf herself, were less extreme than Bell in their wish to abstract art from all representation and content, though they both agreed that the temptation to clutter fiction with a depiction of superficialities such as manners and morals was to be resisted. For a useful introduction to the ideas of Fry and Bell, see Watney (1983).

There was much discussion within Bloomsbury circles as to similarities and distinctions between writing and painting as art forms. Charles Mauron, in *The Nature of Beauty in Art and Literature* (1927), attempted to theorize the application of Fry's ideas to literature. Virginia Woolf herself speculated about some of the issues involved in letters to a painter friend, Jacques Raverat, in 1924-5 (see Bell, 1972). Although there was a habit of referring to her experimental writings as 'impressionist', encouraged by her own phrases in her essay 'Modern Fiction', it seems more helpful, in thinking about the analogy between her novels and painting, to think in terms of Post-Impressionism. This is because of their high degree of formal composition or design, which in some respects produces a textual surface which is not straightforwardly representational but which calls attention to itself as a fabricated and designed object. The discussions about writing and painting in Bloomsbury are examined in Dianne Gillespie's book (1988) about Woolf and her sister, the painter Vanessa Bell.

An early book about Bloomsbury, J.K. Johnstone (1954), discussed Bloomsbury aesthetics in some detail, with a long exposition of Fry's and Mauron's ideas. He claims that Woolf looked at the novel in much the same way that Fry looked at painting. Just as Fry wanted to expel from painting any moral or political content so, Johnstone argues, Woolf kept her art pure of all contamination by her mundane political concerns. Feminism is, he claims, entirely excluded from her novels. Few would now agree with that judgement. A more recent, and far more sophisticated, treatment of these issues is Allen McLaurin's extensive study of the relation between the ideas of Fry and Woolf, *Virginia Woolf: The Echoes Enslaved*. McLaurin draws a parallel between Fry's rejection of photographic representation in visual art and Woolf's attack on 'materialism' in her essays. McLaurin's views, however, are not based only on a comparison of Woolf's programmatic pronouncements in her essays, with Fry's abstract discussions of aesthetics, but more valuably on an examination of Woolf's fiction. His idea is not just to see what she had to say about representation and its limits, but to see how she actually went about it. What kinds of complex, signifying relations between the elements of her fictional worlds, over and above those that arose from realist representation, did she weave into her text? As Fry asserted, the point of art is not to copy or imitate reality but to create other realities, of colour or words, within which forms or patterns not otherwise open to contemplation become visible or audible. The artist achieves this by establishing a system of relationships and McLaurin aims to reveal which systems of relationships, specifically of rhythm and repetition, Woolf composed in her work. He examines, in particular, her use of colour, which he finds to be quite original and analogous with that to be found in Post-Impressionist painting. Colour is used to establish what Mauron called 'psychological volume'. His study of 'repetition' broadens the discussion to bring in a study of work by Lawrence, Dorothy Richardson, Kierkegaard and Bergson.

Perhaps the most useful discussion of these issues is that by David Dowling in his *Bloomsbury Aesthetics and the Novels of Forster and Woolf.* He investigates not only the significance of Bloomsbury aesthetics for our understanding of Woolf, but also her relationship with, and her similarities to and differences from E.M. Forster. Of the two of them, Woolf was closer in her opinions and her art to Fry and Bell. Forster was unwilling to elevate the aesthetic above other aspects of art, and his novels were much more immediately grounded in problems of morality, of personal development and material life than were Woolf's. Their respectful but cool relationship reached a low point in that period in the 1920s when she was writing her most formalist, modernist novels. Dowling brings together their published and unpublished remarks about each other's work.

The painter Lily Briscoe in *To the Lighthouse* seems to produce an abstract painting. Her musing on questions of aesthetics is often taken to be a representation of Woolf's own thoughts on the subject, and is usually identified as a Bloomsbury, formalist view of art. By choosing a self-conscious painter who could ruminate on the principles of her art in such terms that allowed it at the same time to act as a self-examination by the novel itself, Virginia Woolf was able to display for her readers her allegiance to a view of art that was very close to that of Roger Fry. The terms of his best known title, *Vision and Design*, sum up very exactly the terms in which Lily Briscoe explains her own ambitions in her painting, and celebrates her achievement at the end of the novel when she exclaims, 'I have had my vision'. Dowling argues that Woolf owes a major debt to Fry. He argues that *To the Lighthouse* expresses Fry's idea of art as the containment of a fleeting vision, captured or stabilized within the design of the work, and striking the viewer or reader with the contrast to the flow of life and time in which we are otherwise immersed.

This view of *To the Lighthouse* is challenged by Thomas Matro (1984). He argues that the significant terms, 'vision', 'unity', 'oneness' and so on, in terms of which both the aims of art and of the ideals of human relationships are expressed

in the novel, change their meaning in the course of the novel,
as Lily comes to accept the limitations of what is possible both
in life and in art. Lily learns that unity, in the sense of
merging or identity with another person, is impossible. Our
knowledge of other people is always a matter of holding
together a multitude of contrasting and even contradictory
views. There is no resolution. The unity of Lily's painting,
just like the unity of the novel itself, and like the pattern of
human relations, all have to be understood not as coexistence
but as a pattern of connection and separation, of closeness
and distance. The idea expressed by Mrs Ramsay and Lily in
the novel, that one should and can transfix the moment, to
make something permanent of it is, claims Matro, not Woolf's
own ideal, as is usually assumed, but is treated by Woolf
ironically. In the end, Woolf is not concerned with the impossible task of making time stand still, but with capturing
the very processes of the mind, the ways that meanings are
formed and destroyed, the ways that simple human needs for
sympathy and communication, for seeing and loving, are
performed. Matro's argument is that the irony has been
missed in the dominant critical approach to the novel, which
has mistakenly taken it to be at one with Fry's Post-Impressionist aesthetic.

Johnson (1987) discusses Woolf's relation to modernism,
which she identifies with the aesthetics of Bell and Fry. She
examines, though at a damagingly high level of generality,
the relations between feminism, Bloomsbury modernism and
postmodernism.

3

Virginia Woolf and Modernism

Modernist Culture

The international culture of modernism as a broad literary movement is discussed in the compendious volume edited by Bradbury and McFarlane (1976). In their Introduction the editors sketch in the immense maze of modernist literature and posit it as an aesthetic response to a more general crisis in modern culture arising from the experience of the modern world. They speculate as to the reasons why, after roughly 1890, conventional forms of expression in fiction, poetry, painting and music no longer served. The crisis is located in many institutions, in the family, religion and morality, in government, in the social role of women, in the relations between the classes, and so on. It is intriguing to view Woolf in this broad international perspective, and interesting to note that she is presented as a somewhat minor figure in this movement, receiving only half the space devoted to such as Joyce and Eliot. It is undoubtedly true that we gain a quite different view of her work in this perspective than we do when it is approached via psychobiographical speculation or through its relations more narrowly with Bloomsbury. Her main appearance in the volume is in the chapter by Melvin Friedman on the symbolist novel. Here her modernism is defined in terms of the fact that she is not concerned with conventional features of fiction such as story, linearity, character and life story, but with fragments of experience which, no longer connected up in conventional ways, are reconnected with one another through repeated images and symbols. Her work is compared with that of Faulkner and Malraux in these respects.

Many of the general points which are made in this volume are repeated in Bradbury (1989), in which Woolf appears as one (the only woman) of the 'ten great writers' of the modern world. This book was conceived as a tie-in with a British television series and therefore had a potential audience of far greater magnitude and far broader range than any of the academic studies mentioned in this present book. One might think that this would produce a special responsibility to be clear, accurate and informative as to the impulses and central purposes of the great writers and thereby to win for them a wide audience. Unfortunately, the book is not, in my view, a successful response to this challenge. There is one chapter on Virginia Woolf and it focuses on *Mrs Dalloway*. Bradbury's approach agrees with that of Zwerdling in perceiving the connection between Woolf's fascination with the subtleties of consciousness and her wish to depict and criticize social relations and historical process. She was responding to a very specific historical situation in the 1920s, and her novel is modern both in that it is a response to these features of the modern world and in its resulting modern technique. Bradbury's efforts to characterize the modernist form of her novel never quite succeed. He emphasizes that she depicts experience as fragmentary, in an 'impressionist' style, with a weaving of symbolist reconnections between the fragments in an effort to reveal deep themes and meanings. But his account is careless and slapdash: he asserts that she was born and brought up in Bloomsbury which she emphatically was not; he invents a biography of her by Clive Bell which does not exist, and his bibliography on Woolf mentions only two books published since 1970 and nothing published since 1979. He has not taken the opportunity to go back to the text and to catch up on critical debates, and it is a sad failure to reach out to a potentially very large audience.

David Lodge (1977) sees modernism as resulting from a shift from realist (or metonymic) to symbolist (or metaphoric) representation of experience. Literary modernism might be seen as a short-lived experiment that never took deep root in English literary culture and was already under attack as elitist and obscure in the 1930s. Alternatively, and this is Lodge's preferred view, there has been a constant war since the 1930s between 'realism' and 'modernism'. Lodge is concerned with the trajectory of modernism in its heroic phase. He traces the developing modernism of Woolf's work from *The Voyage Out* to *The Waves*. He neglects all her later work, seeing *The Waves* as the 'logical terminus' of her development. This is a view which would be disputed by many critics, particularly those who would wish to emphasize her liberation from the more formalist aspects of modernism in her later work. He provides a brief analysis of each of her novels within this framework and compares her work with that of other modernist authors. In her work there is a progressive disappearance of traditional elements of the novel, of rounded characters, logically articulated plot, solidly specified setting, and narrator's commentary (which is replaced by discourse from characters' points of view). There is concomitantly an increasing unification of the texts by repeated symbols and motifs. Her writing aspired to the condition of lyrical poetry and her aim was to affirm, even in the face of death, the value of life and its moments of special joy. Lodge points out the similarity between Woolf's moments of being and Joyce's 'epiphanies', though his account of the latter is imprecise and leaves one wishing for a more specialist treatment, such as that by Beja (1971). He points out the difference between Woolf and authors such as Eliot and Yeats, for whom moments of special revelation are interpreted in terms of some particular metaphysic. Lodge argues that Woolf's scepticism or relativism, her unwillingness to force privileged moments to yield up answers to the fundamental questions of life and death, undermines the redeeming power of these moments, for they are never shared but have only individual, personal meaning. One might have thought that, on the contrary, in this refusal to allow that our interrogation of life can arrive at a settled conclusion, Virginia Woolf was being more rigorously modern than Lodge's preferred authors. Lodge's view seems to be that the affirmation of life does not count if it is based only on the value of special moments, unless they are conceived in some way that could provide a shared, public meaning for our experiences. It is hard to see why this should be so. This book is a useful starting point and its main virtue is that it gives a view of Woolf in the context of modernist literary culture, but it lacks a detailed technical analysis of the formal aspects of her work. For that we must look to the works discussed in the next section.

For Woolf's relations, personal and literary, with some other modern authors, see her *Diary*. In addition, for T.S. Eliot, with whom she was a friend for many years, see Peter Ackroyd (1984) and Lyndall Gordon (1983). Woolf had a shorter, but intense, and competitive acquaintance with Katherine Mansfield, who was six years her junior but who died in 1923: see Jeffrey Meyers (1978, pp.136-48). This book also provides a useful portrait of literary London in the period 1910-20, with its social network of writers and small magazine publication. Woolf never met Joyce, but her reading of and comments upon his work are important. Henig's '*Ulysses* in Bloomsbury' (1973) and Henke (1986) tell the story of Woolf's fluctuating responses to *Ulysses* and to the possibility of publishing *Ulysses* at the Hogarth Press. Maria DiBattista's 'Joyce, Woolf and the Modern Mind' is very good on the literary parallels between *Ulysses* (and specifically 'The Wandering Rocks') and *Mrs Dalloway*.

Many of the above approaches to modernism highlight such themes as alienation, fragmentation and discontinuity on the one hand, and the move away from narrative continuity and towards symbolic or metaphoric meaning on the other. The effort to fit Virginia Woolf into this framework sometimes seems rather forced. This is so partly because in her work alienation and disconnection between people are counterbalanced by a kind of faith in the possibilities of connection, of being 'we' instead of 'I', if only at some impersonal level. Moreover, some attempts to elucidate the positive significance of her symbolism and metaphor (her 'poetic prose') are rather weak. Differences between authors seem more compelling than their similarities. Whatever Joyce achieved through 'myth' and repetition in *Ulysses*, this novel seems in spirit very unlike *To the Lighthouse* or *The Waves*.

Several attempts to identify common ground among some at least of the modern novelists have focused on the prioritization of saturated or poetic meaning over narrative and character. In Woolf's work this is connected with the centrality of the idea of 'vision' or 'revelation'. Beja's *Epiphany in the Modern Novel* (1971) discusses those modern authors who place great emphasis on the idea of specially revealing or meaningful moments of experience, moments in which some truth or aspect of reality is condensed or shown forth (moments which Joyce called 'epiphanies'). The comparison with Joyce focuses, in this perspective, not on the linguistic and narrative self-consciousness of *Ulysses* but on his earlier works (for the idea of epiphany has little place in his work after *Portrait*). Beja's book brings together a wide range of European fiction identified not in terms of modernist or avant-garde technique but in terms of the focus on 'epiphany'. He has chapters on Joyce, Woolf, Thomas Wolfe and Faulkner, as well as on more recent authors. For 'epiphany', he argues, like 'stream of consciousness' technique and interior monologue, has become part of the modern literary tradition.

In his chapter on Woolf he collects together many of her references (in her diaries and her essays, in 'A Sketch of the Past' and in her novels, most obviously *Mrs Dalloway* and *To the Lighthouse*), to the theme of moments of vision or revelation. He discusses their significance, for they do indeed seem very important to both the form and the content of her work. Beja argues that these moments, which are not great revelations answering all our questions but are little miracles or illuminations in which we seem to come wordlessly face to face with Being, determine the character and structure of her novels. It is because they are her main target that her novels have all the modernist features observed by Lodge and others. The novels are not primarily designed as vehicles for

story-telling but as ways of representing moments of being.
Hence the lack of plot and character and hence also everything about them that people sum up in the word 'poetic' (or
'symbolic'). As to Woolf's understanding of these moments,
her answer to the question as to what it is that these revelations in fact reveal, Beja rightly observes that she could not
make up her mind. Perhaps life is solid; perhaps time does
not exist; perhaps there is an underlying pattern or reality
obscured by all the shifting, fleeting movement of life. She
certainly often seemed to believe so. Yet there are other diary
entries in which she expresses uncertainty. Her ruminations
connect her thinking with some of the main streams of
modern European thought – on time and memory, on the
unconscious, on the ways in which our past experience is
strangely stored up, often in non-verbal forms and sometimes
only retrievable in involuntary streams of recollection. The
similarities with, and possible influence of, Proust are obvious. Moreover, Beja points out, Woolf's main characters are
often, like their author, both emphatically non-religious and
yet intensely spiritual, and this has led some commentators
to use of her the word 'mystical', a word which Beja finds
inaccurate and which underestimates the extent of her materialism. The view that Woolf's work is precisely characterized by an idiosyncratic mix of the mystical and the
political is put forth by Moore (1984). Beja also discusses the
similarities between Woolf's view of fiction as based on epiphanies and the views of Bell and Fry on art and significant
form which I have mentioned above.

Another attempt to identify what might be called a school
of 'visionary modernism', in contrast to the modernism of
alienation, can be found in Thickstun's *Visionary Closure in
the Modern Novel*, in which Woolf appears again, though in
rather different company, among a group of authors whose
works generate a positive, and in some cases even prophetic,
meaning. Thickstun points out that between 1910 and 1929
five writers brought novels to a conclusion with a scene in
which a woman has a visionary experience, and he sets
himself the task of elucidating the meaning of these culminating moments of vision. The five novels are Forster's

Howards End, Lawrence's *The Rainbow*, Joyce's *Ulysses*, Woolf's *To the Lighthouse* and Faulkner's *The Sound and the Fury*. Some of the moments of visionary closure at the end of these novels have a prophetic quality, whether anxious, as in Forster, or utopian and affirmative, as in Lawrence. In others, such as Woolf, there is a puzzle as to whether the closure stems only from an aesthetic demand, which leaves all questions of human life and destiny unresolved, or whether the experience depicted should be understood as in some way redemptive. We are back to the question raised above: 'What does significant form signify?' As Thickstun puts it, is there some conflict between the demands of aestheic form, which requires closure, and the aim of psychological verisimilitude, truth to the perpetual openness of experience, which points rather to the need for ending without closure? Is there anything distinctively modern about modern visionary endings?

As for *To the Lighthouse,* Thickstun claims that the culminating moment of vision 'irradiates and transforms the novel as a whole, changing its fabric into a thin veil through which we glimpse, fleetingly but unmistakably, a world beyond our own'. Time is shown as having the power not only to destroy but also to heal. The special moment, the moment of vision, is a moment of intersection of eternity with daily life, offering the possibility of reassembling the scattered fragments of life into a new resolved order of meaning. Thickstun's reading lifts into central significance a moment in Part III of *To the Lighthouse* which is rarely commented on by the critics, for most comment is directed to Lily's painting and not to the vision which it captures. That vision is of Mrs Ramsay. At one moment Lily looks up at the house and sees Mrs Ramsay, dead now ten years: 'There she sat.' Thickstun insists that although we resist it we should take this as a declaration of Mrs Ramsay's presence and, therefore, if we can allow ourselves to trust the vision, as the transcendence of transcience and death. Thickstun's reading, more than any other, pushes the interpretation of Woolf in a religious direction.

Modernist Forms

Broad definitions of modernism tend to be hopelessly vague when it comes to the analysis of specific authors' techniques. It is all very well saying that modern authors shift from metonymic to metaphoric use of language or that Woolf's prose is symbolist or poetic, but these descriptions are far too ill-defined to act as serious precision tools in the analysis of style. Equally, it is hopeless to rely on Woolf's own ideas about the distinctive subject matter or style of 'modern fiction', taken from her essay of that title. This essay was first published before she had written any of her own distinctively modernist novels (i.e., long before she developed her characteristic techniques for representing consciousness). What is needed is not repeated quotation of the same passages from her essays but conceptual clarification and detailed textual analysis. We need to know what exactly it is that she was intending to achieve in her unconventional novels, and how exactly – by means of precisely what technical means – she accomplished it. Careful, detailed work of this kind is available in the following three books: by Erich Auerbach (1953), by Erwin Steinberg (1979) and by Dorrit Cohn (1978).

Perhaps the single best known discussion of Virginia Woolf as an exemplary modern writer is also one of the earliest. In Erich Auerbach's *Mimesis: The Representation of Reality in Western Literature*, published in German in 1946 and in English in 1953, one passage is selected from *To the Lighthouse* for very detailed scrutiny and eventually as yielding up an interpretation of the modern representation of reality in literature. It was the first time that this high status of representative of her age had been conferred on Woolf.

Trapped in Istanbul during the war, an escapee from the Nazis, with only a limited personal library available to him, Auerbach set himself the ambitious task of surveying and analysing, in the words of his sub-title, the techniques for 'the representation of reality in western literature', starting with Homer and the Bible and proceeding step by patient step all the way up to the modern period. His celebrated chapter 'The Brown Stocking' was a turning point in Woolf criticism, for here she was no longer taken to be a baffling member of the 1920s avant-garde, of disputable merit and specializing in the hypersensitive, impressionistic depiction of consciousness. She was now presented as the representative figure of her age who, in her innovative technique, had discovered a way of articulating the central themes of life in Europe in the period following the First World War. Auerbach's approach is characterized by the minuteness and meticulousness of his technical analysis and the way in which he then draws on his results to speculate on the broader cultural significance of her innovations in literary form.

His method rests on his very detailed analysis of a single passage, one in which Mrs Ramsay is shown knitting as she sits with her son James. He demonstrates that the narration cannot be understood simply as the representation of a stream of consciousness, though it does include that, for it does not follow a single fictional consciousness. It shifts subtly from one consciousness to another, from Mrs Ramsay to Mr Bankes, and then to an anonymous collective consciousness. Furthermore, the narrative is not a stream of consciousness because it does not follow consciousness continuously in time but shifts backwards and forwards in fictional time, and dips into time's stream at widely separated points. A third relevant feature of the narration is that its status is ambiguous. It seems to be the representation of the contents of the minds of the characters, yet it cannot always be read in that way. It sometimes seems oddly suspended between two different points of view, that of a narrator and that of a character. It is neither simply narrator's commentary nor is it the quotation of characters' thoughts, but both simultaneously. It is, grammatically speaking, neither direct nor indirect speech, but that odd fusion of them known as 'free indirect speech'. The question 'Who speaks? Whose words are these?', which Auerbach raised in relation to this passage from *To the Lighthouse*, has been puzzling and exciting critics and theorists ever since. In Woolf's case, it became clear, the point of her very distinctive prose is lost if one lazily regards it only as recording a stream of consciousness. Her sentences are carefully composed so as to present fragments of characters' consciousness while also surrounding each such fragment with a semantic context. This builds up a complex network of associations and semantic connections. Hence there is great density or saturation of meaning. Each moment derives its meaning from other textual moments: some associations derive from points which are remote in time in the character's subjective life, others derive from the streams of consciousness of other characters, and still others from the narrator's composed symbolic framework and repetitions of theme and image. This extremely complex composition has the effect of bringing to bear on each apparently trivial detail of a character's experience a wealth of associations. Meaning is condensed in images, sometimes of great power, which are not derived from the character's own stream of consciousness. The work of the narration, like dream work, draws enigmatic unconscious material into a network of overdetermined images. Auerbach sums up his results in the following phrases: there is multipersonal representation of consciousness with synthesis as its aim (which is to say that knowledge emerges as the synthesis of many points of view); there is omnitemporality (i.e., the co-presence in consciousness of episodes and events from different points in time, deriving significance not from their position in an objective time series but from the relations between experiences distant in time); and there is a narrator who lacks omniscience, and a reality of which no complete and objective knowledge is possible. The narrator's position of authority has been abdicated.

These devices are the symptoms of attitudes which Woolf shared with other authors, and Auerbach sees them as reactions to modernity which can be found also in Proust, Joyce, Knut Hamsun and Thomas Mann. For Auerbach, modern fiction is thought of not in terms of the play of language and the metafictional features that are so prominent in *Ulysses* but as a strand of psychological realism which was dedicated to the representation of the mind in relation to time and memory. The emphasis is no longer on exterior events and narratives of the public world, as it had been in the great 19th-century novels. It is rather on random fragments of subjective life which can be made, by cunningly organized narration, to yield up a synthesized view of character and of a life, as the fragment of a fossil bone can be made by cunning scientific reconstruction to yield up the anatomy of a whole extinct species of organism. Public ideologies in modern European societies elicit among their writers nothing but scepticism and isolation. This had been as true in the aftermath of the First World War as it was when Auerbach was writing in the middle of the Second World War. It was a time of violently clashing and fiercely assertive public discourses, of fascism and communism, in which modern writers could have no faith. For Proust, Joyce and Woolf meaning resided elsewhere. Though some of the details of Auerbach's analyses have, of course, been revised or challenged, his agenda has not been rejected, as we can see both in the diagnoses of modernist culture above and in the more technical research into modernist forms to which I will now turn.

Erwin Steinberg's *The Stream-of-Consciousness Technique in the Modern Novel* is a helpful collection of readings and commentary. It brings together passages that give the history of the idea of the 'stream of consciousness', its source in the psychology of William James and the philosophy of Bergson, and its early use in authors such as Dorothy Richardson, Proust, Joyce, Woolf and Faulkner. Most of the book presents material which aims at clarifying and refining the idea sufficiently to make of it a usable analytical tool. The editor surveys and comments on rival theories and definitions. Much of the muddle about the 'stream of consciousness' derives from the fact that it is not the name of a particular literary technique (for a large and confusing variety of quite different techniques have been referred to using the term). It is rather the name of a range of very complex psychological phenomena. The psychological complexity of consciousness and its contents means that there is no single well-defined technique or device for representing it. The kinds of mental contents which are part of the stream of consciousness are extremely varied and include everything from well-ordered, articulated thoughts to mental images, sensations and disjointed sequences of feeling and emotion. There can be many kinds of 'stream-of-consciousness' fiction depending on which among all of these elements are the main subject matter. No form of fiction, no unilinear verbal chain, can hope to encompass it all and each author's attempts to render consciousness in words assumes a difference of selection and emphasis. This gives rise to an extensive range of different literary techniques, styles and effects, all of which need to be analysed and distinguished carefully. Unfortunately there is, in English, no single accepted vocabulary for describing the variety of these linguistic techniques and the student will encounter widespread confusion of terms. Steinberg's book provides guidance here and offers some clarification of the different terms and techniques, such as soliloquy, interior monologue, *erlebte Rede*, and so on.

Perhaps the single most important point in the discussion is this, that fiction does not and cannot *reproduce*, as in a copy, the 'stream of consciousness', the flow of mental contents. The most obvious reason for this is that many kinds of mental activity are not verbal in form; not even all thought is verbal thought, and not everything in consciousness is thought. The non-verbal material in consciousness cannot be 'presented', in the sense of 'quoted', in language; it can only be somehow simulated, if an author can find some plausible verbal equivalents. Unfortunately, a great deal of commentary on the task that fiction sets itself in recording the contents of consciousness, including Woolf's own stumbling formulations in 'Modern Fiction', do suggest that fiction could be some kind of passive recording of a sequence of mental events in words, whereas it must, in fact, be a creative rendering of these events through the artifice of verbal invention and convention.

A second reason why this must be so, over and above the fact that the mental contents are often crucially not verbal in form, is that they are not unilinear or sequential in form either. At each instant the contents of consciousness are enormously complex. They are not 'atoms', but have complex internal structure. As Steinberg argues, the structure of language differs from the structure of the world. Reality, including the reality of consciousness, is multidimensional at each instant, not atomistic. Consciousness is not a stream of 'atoms' or 'impressions' – the words Woolf herself used in 'Modern Fiction' to characterize consciousness, though she also declared it to be like a 'luminous halo'. None of these metaphors come close to accurately capturing the particular forms of complexity of consciousness, and Woolf herself later dropped them.

Her efforts to explore the non-stream-like complexity of consciousness are best followed not in her essays but in her fiction, though there is one particular piece, printed with her essays, in which she directly tackles the problem. This is 'The Moment: Summer's Night', and it is taken by Harvena Richter (1970) as a key text for the analysis of Woolf's ideas about consciousness and its contents. Richter's book approaches the topic from a philosophical point of view (and I discuss it under that rubric below) rather than from that of literary technique, and it is the most detailed specialist work on the topic of Woolf's views on subjectivity. Another useful discussion is James Naremore's chapter 'Virginia Woolf and the Stream of Consciousness' (1973). Naremore points out that discussion of Woolf's technique is confused not only because critics have understated the psychological complexity of the stream of consciousness but also because they have tended to leave out the fact that her intentions were not limited to psychological realism: she wanted also to render something beyond consciousness, something transcendent. To discuss her techniques only from the point of view of the representation of subjectivity is to miss this crucial dimension of her work.

In summary, the discussion of the techniques of modernist novelists must take account of the fact that each novelist finds his or her own way of rendering only selected aspects of these varied and complex mental phenomena. The results, of course, vary greatly: for example, think of Joyce's representation of Molly Bloom's interior speech in *Ulysses*, Knut Hamsun's first-person reverie in *Hunger*, Woolf's soliloquies in *The Waves*, and her 'tunnelling' technique for representing the pressure of memory in the present moment in *Mrs Dalloway*. It is important not to blur the differences between these inventive forms of writing, not to underestimate their authors' achievements, by employing an oversimple critical vocabulary.

I move on now to look at linguistic studies of Woolf's work, by which I mean attempts to bring linguistic and grammatical·analysis to bear on the problem of characterizing her style. Unfortunately, this kind of work is not common in English, though German scholars have made a speciality of it. There is, however, one major work to which we can turn in English. This is Dorrit Cohn's *Transparent Minds: Narrative Modes for Presenting Consciousness in Fiction*, which contains a great deal of discussion of Virginia Woolf. Cohn's study carefully discriminates the varieties of narrative form in modern fiction and includes detailed analysis of passages from *Mrs Dalloway*, *To the Lighthouse* and *The Waves*. Great analytical precision is derived from the book's conceptual framework, which suggests a typology of modes of presenting consciousnesss in six categories – three in first-person and three in third-person fiction. The latter three forms are labelled 'Psycho-Narration', 'Quoted Monologue' and 'Narrated Monologue'. Each exhibits important sub-varieties and they can all be found in interesting combinations in particular texts. 'Narrated Monologue' is perhaps the most fascinating form. It is significant of the neglect of this kind of formal analysis in English that there is no agreed and stable vocabulary for these linguistic forms. 'Narrated Monologue' is what in other works is sometimes referred to as *erlebte Rede*, *style indirecte libre*, free indirect speech, or quasi-direct discourse. It is defined by Cohn as character's mental discourse in the guise of narrator's discourse.

The characteristic feel of Woolf's prose in *Mrs Dalloway* and *To the Lighthouse* can be traced to her particular way of combining and moving between these three modes of presenting consciousness. It is a movement that typically represents a subtle shift of attention from the surface, conscious contents of the mind to layers of mental material and activity that are non-verbalized and no more than sub-conscious. It is a stylistic technique in sharp contrast to that which she uses in *The Waves*. Cohn gives a very precise and illuminating analysis of this latter technique – a highly unusual form of autonomous monologue. She shows how, with this technique, Woolf pushed the linguistic features of prose fiction to the limit; for, grammatically speaking, this work converges with dramatic monologue and prose poem. It is revealed clearly that, from a technical point of view, *The Waves* is a cul-de-sac: this is not a direction in which fiction could develop. The scientific basis of Cohn's book makes possible great advances in clarity in areas of analysis which had previously been in a very murky and impressionistic state.

4

Feminist Studies

A Passionate Audience

Feminist studies of Woolf are often distinguished not only by particular theoretical or conceptual instruments but also by a tone of passionate commitment, different from that of professional detachment. It is not unusual for feminist scholars to comment explicitly upon the significance their work has in their lives. They view it not just in terms of a career or a general commitment to literary scholarship but in relation to their own most urgent and exciting self-questioning. Investigating as a woman can mean using research as a way of clarifying what it is to be a woman, and what it is for a woman to be a writer. Researching Woolf's work connects here with more general questions of identity and political struggle. For these reasons, much of the writing about Woolf by feminist critics has a pugnacious and passionate tone, and also sometimes a confessional quality, that mark it off from more mainstream academic work.

For example, one cannot, unfortunately, imagine a group of male scholars getting together to produce a volume like that edited by Ascher, DeSalvo and Ruddick (1984). In this book both Sara Ruddick and Louise DeSalvo write in a confessional and autobiographical manner about how they came to be Woolf scholars and about how they view their work as deeply connected with the most essential themes of their own life-narratives (marriage, children, family, politics and so on). Clearly, Virginia Woolf has been inspirational for them. Sara Ruddick writes: 'Woolf inspired me to find...myself. I am not sure how she conferred this gift of self-recovery.... Time and again, students, writing with grateful astonishment of the ways Woolf enhances and deepens their lives, remind me of this mysterious gift of authenticity Woolf confers' (p.142). Carolyn Heilbrun's *Writing a Woman's Life* is another example: she challenges the norms of autobiographical and biographical writing from a feminist perspective, inspired by the example of Virginia Woolf, showing the connection between literary problems (writing life stories) and existential problems (life choices).

It is as if women critics have rediscovered, or have the courage explicitly to proclaim and defend, the positive cognitive and existential purposes of literature. The volume edited by Nancy Miller (1986) records the proceedings of a colloquium on the poetics of gender held at Columbia University in 1984, an event at which, as Carolyn Heilbrun remarks in the Foreword, Virginia Woolf was mentioned more often than any other author. It was, contributors remark, a passionate event with a passionate audience. Woolf's influence has been to empower women academics, helping them to set their agendas, and has given them the courage to define their own areas of research. It has provided women with a sense of community and of their place in a tradition. Not the least of Woolf's contributions was her postulation that there has been a tradition of women's writing, that modern women writers can think back through their mothers. Her example now leads others to challenge the definition of the literary canon, the lists of prescribed great works that are required reading for students. Among the most forceful in her claims in this area has been Jane Marcus in her various books. She points out, perhaps most explicitly in her 'Introduction' to *Art and Anger* (1988), that her writings have revolutionary aims. Her project is to force the questions raised in *A Room of One's Own* and *Three Guineas* onto the agenda of literary work in the academy. This is conceived as part of a broader radical project, to 'change the subject', by which she means changing the canon, changing interpretations, changing the values and ends of literary work, and promoting the powerfully subversive sense of a female literary tradition. See also her combative discourse on solidarity and struggle, on the revolutionary quality of Woolf's work in both form and content, in *Virginia Woolf: A Feminist Slant* (1983).

Woolf's Feminist Theory

Virginia Woolf's most important contributions to feminist thinking are to be found in *A Room of One's Own*, *Three Guineas*, and the essays 'Women and Fiction' and 'Professions for Women'. In *A Room of One's Own* she highlights questions about writing as a woman, for example: What are the obstacles to a woman's writing? Is there a specifically female literary tradition which would enable women writers to 'think back through their mothers'? Are women's values and women's use of language different from men's? Perhaps the most debated of Woolf's ideas in that book is that ideally a writer should be androgynous, should in some sense combine manly and womanly qualities.

As many authors have pointed out, Woolf seems on the face of it to contradict herself in *A Room of One's Own*. For much of the book she seems to argue that women should write as women, in a gender-specific way. Yet towards the end of the book she argues that, when writing, a woman should be unconscious of her sex and should be open to both the manly and the womanly aspects of herself. She must be impersonal, putting aside all personal anger and grievance. So the climax of Woolf's argument, the invocation of the ideal of the androgynous writer, seems to undercut all that has gone before in which gender was systematically highlighted. Woolf's assertion of the ideal of 'androgyny' has given rise to some of the most important and heated debate about her work.

In the early 1970s two influential works endorsed the idea of androgyny and took it to be central to an interpretation of Woolf's fiction. Nancy Topping Bazin (1973) put forward a psychological interpretation of the ideal of androgyny according to which it was rooted in Woolf's personal manic-depressive psychological history. The manic phase is seen as associated with her mother, and by extension with the feminine gender. This is, moreover, associated with a belief in an underlying design or pattern in reality, from which life derives its meaning. The depressive phase is seen as associated with her father, and by extension with the masculine gender. This is, moreover, conceived as characterized by a scientific, rational view of life as a meaningless, material flux. The unstable and fluctuating swings from one of these poles to the other, which characterize the manic-depressive personality, are seen as deriving from emotional disturbance. They are a form of pathology. Androgyny is interpreted as an ideal balance between these two forces. Bazin's book interprets eight of Woolf's novels in terms of this scheme (oddly, it is *Orlando* which is left out). Each book is analysed as arising from Woolf's quest for an equilibrium between two views of life (life is seen as shifting and unstable, or it is seen as built upon something solid and permanent). Woolf's life and career are seen in terms of her struggle to find harmony between her opposing tendencies, to find a lost sense of wholeness.

Carolyn Heilbrun's *Towards Androgyny* (1973) is not specifically a study of Virginia Woolf but is the statement of a cultural project, the desire to move towards a world in which gender roles are not pre-ordained or socially imposed but in which individuals can freely choose their modes of behaviour and social lives. The ideal of androgyny on this view is that of the liberation of individuals from the constraints of imposed masculinity or femininity. It is not an equilibrium of different genders but a denial of difference. The book hunts out the expression of this ideal in literature and myth. In Part 2, Heilbrun discusses the Bloomsbury Group as the living personification of this ideal (note Phyllis Rose's opposed interpretation of the Bloomsbury Group, mentioned in a later section of this chapter). She also presents an interpretation of *To the Lighthouse* in which she argues that contrary to the views of most previous critics, Mrs Ramsay is not Woolf's ideal of womanhood, for she is not androgynous. She is feminine in an unbalanced way and is therefore one-sided and life-denying just as much as her husband. Both the Ramsays' marriage and that of the Dalloways in *Mrs Dallo-way* are failures and are life-denying compared with the life-enhancing 'marriage of the future' at the end of *Orlando*.

An influential negative view of Woolf's feminist writing can be found in Elaine Showalter's *A Literature of their Own* (1978). Showalter's book is very much in the Woolfian tradition of providing a gendered view of literary history, which means specifically attempting to rescue from neglect the great mass of women's fiction from 1800 to the present day, and trying to understand the history of that writing, the changes in the ways in which women have used writing over that period. What kinds of voice have women writers created for themselves in their fiction? In relation to Woolf she asks not only about the content of her feminist polemical works but also about their rhetorical strategy. How does Woolf go about attempting to persuade her readers to take her arguments seriously? In *A Room of One's Own* Woolf attempts to disguise the anger and resentment she feels in relation to the obstacles put in the way of a woman's education and writing. She chooses to create a seductive, charming persona, a voice that is witty and calm and which will not be felt as threatening by her male readers. She wishes to examine women's oppression by men without antagonizing the men in her audience. Above all she wishes to assert the importance of avoiding anger in fiction and shows how an author's anger can deform and spoil her writing. A woman must repress her sense of grievance. In Showalter's view this denial of anger is itself a negative, distorting feature of Woolf's prose, for it produces an uneasily defensive and evasive smoothness, a false sense of playfulness. This is not the result of a healthy control of her own feelings but of a damaged female identity, for Woolf had not achieved a secure sense of herself as a woman. Woolf's strongly felt need for 'a room of her own', in which she could escape the interference of men and hope to overcome her own training in deference to men, reflects her history of uncertainty and irresolution in relation to her own identity.

Similarly, her ideal of androgyny reflects her felt need to integrate the different warring aspects of her own personality. But, argues Showalter, these metaphors are ambiguous. We can see the room of her own as a prison rather than a sanctuary, and we can see androgyny as a metaphor for sexlessness and sterility rather than for fruitful consummation and integrity. Both can be regarded as deriving from a denial of real and powerful feelings rather than a healthy mastery of them. Woolf was embarrassed by and frightened of her anger. She could not bring herself to own it for fear of alienating her men friends. This is the reason why, in the end, her argument turns away from its feminist themes and seeks a retreat in the transcendental. She seeks to escape from the battleground of personal emotions and the turbulance of personal desires and needs, to find peace in a realm of transcendental significance. This move is indicated by her ideal of androgyny, and is most explicitly expressed in 'Women and Fiction' and 'The Narrow Bridge of Art'. She turns from feminism to mysticism and thus escapes from those parts of herself that she never managed to confront without panic – her body, her passions, her sexuality. Thus androgyny, in this reading, is not a feminist concept but a denial of her feminist anger and an attempt to escape from her alienation from her own body.

In the 1930s Woolf struggled to overcome her reticence in relation to her anger and to liberate herself from her fear of men's reactions to her opinions. This she attempted in *The Pargiters*, *Three Guineas* and *The Years*, though not, says Showalter, ultimately successfully. *Three Guineas* is an angry book and it refuses the falsely charming and seductive posture of *A Room of One's Own*. It is a fierce denunciation of men's desire to dominate and the violence and destruction to which this gives rise. Yet this book, according to Showalter, once again fails to describe her own experience. It is again ruined by its attempted impersonality, its evasiveness, its rhetorical trickery. It is courageous but it rings false. Her problem may be not only her incapacity to be open about the roots of her own resentments, but also her class position, which resulted in her being isolated from the mainstream of women's experience. Her privileged, moneyed and cultured life cut her off from the experience of the majority of women, even of those 'daughters of educated men' on whose behalf she claims to speak. The book was savagely attacked in a famously abusive review by Q.D. Leavis in *Scrutiny* (1938), and Showalter is one of the few critics who have been prepared to allow that Leavis might have had an accurate perception of Woolf's difficulties.

A more recent work in the Showalter tradition is Patricia Stubbs' *Women and Fiction* which concludes with a chapter on Woolf. One of Stubbs' themes is the absence of any depiction of female sexuality in the 19th-century novel, an absence that persisted well into the 20th century. Lawrence attempted the task, with the familiar dreadful results, but for women authors it remained a very difficult area. Virginia Woolf found it impossible to tell the truth about women's bodies and passions (as she admitted in 'Professions for Women'). Moreover, women characters in fiction continued to be represented in terms of their emotions and relationships rather than their everyday material lives. Woolf argued in *A Room of One's Own* for a new fiction which would record women's experiences and 'the lives of the obscure', yet she failed to achieve this in her own novels. Picking up on a theme in Showalter, Stubbs argues that Woolf failed to provide new images of women, new models of women's social life or experience, in her fiction. These failures and limitations in Woolf's fiction are seen by Stubbs as related to her ideas as expressed in 'Modern Fiction', with its impressionistic, subjectivist conception of fiction. Because of her emphasis on subjectivity, Woolf neglected the shared, material reality of women's lives. In this essay, says Stubbs, experience is 'mystified almost beyond recognition'. Far from being subversive or liberating in a feminist manner, she says, Woolf's aesthetic theories 'actually devitalised her fictional world'. This failure, her inability to keep her attention concentrated steadily upon the material life and the physical embodiment of women, is the underlying reason for Woolf's flight to androgyny at the end of *A Room of One's Own*. She effectively abandoned the idea of writing as a woman and ruled out the possibility of any 'vigorous quarrel with social orthodoxies'. The Showalter/Stubbs interpretation of the theory of androgyny is fiercely disputed by the poststructuralist feminists (see later). The argument that Woolf failed in her aims to represent women's lives is disputed by Jane Wheare whose book I discuss in ch. 6 later.

Another author who finds that Woolf's polemical work suffers from contradiction is Michèle Barrett (1979). In her summary of Woolf's ideas on women and writing Barrett finds that their strength lies in her materialism. By this she means all those ways in which Woolf recognized and explored the roots of writing in the specific historical contexts of women's lives. Literature is not an airy emanation of some spiritual realm but is anchored firmly in material life, in houses and marriages, in the socially distributed tasks of childrearing and family management, in money or its absence, in access to or deprivation of education, and so on. In *A Room of One's Own* and in her essays on women writers, Woolf wrote many marvellous passages on these material bases of, or obstacles to, literary creation, not least in her celebrated invocation of the tragic figure of Judith Shakespeare. She had a firm sense of the way in which the historical contours of the women's literary tradition had been moulded by their social experience. Her essays on Aphra Behn, the Duchess of Newcastle, Mary Wollstonecraft and others attend to the material conditions of their work and their hard struggle to establish sufficient autonomy and solidity of identity to be able to create distinctive voices for themselves and to explore their distinctively female values.

In a famous argument in *A Room of One's Own* Woolf put forward the idea that an aspect of the women's literary tradition has been the development of a 'women's sentence', some specifically female way of using language. It is an idea that she had already put forward in a review of Dorothy Richardson in which she asserted that Richardson had invented 'the psychological sentence of the feminine gender'. However, this idea, according to Barrett, is also given a historical meaning. The difference between men's and women's writing is not intrinsic but is a consequence of their different conditions of life and the differences in values and subject matter in their fiction.

External constraints on women are not the only obstacles in the way of their careers as writers, for they are also impeded by internal, psychological constraints, internalized norms of behaviour and patterns of feeling that derive from their social life and which stand in the way of their honest and unimpeded exploration of life. These forces Woolf sums up in the figure of the angel in the house, the docile, subservient aspects of female personality which must be killed in order to allow a woman to write freely.

There is, however, according to Barrett, another strand in Woolf's thinking which is in contradiction with and works against this materialist strand. This is Woolf's taste for romantic transcendence, which leads her sometimes to play down the social content and value of art and to see as its highest value its dedication to mystical themes. It is this which leads her to introduce the unsatisfactory idea of androgyny, to assert that the writer should not be conscious of her sex, and that causes her to see a clear division between art, which is impersonal and transcendent, and politics or preaching which are propaganda. In all these doctrines she 'resists the implications of her own materialist position'.

The problem of the relation between the mystical and the material or political in Woolf's work is also central to Madeline Moore's *The Short Season Between Two Silences: The Mystical and the Political in the Novels of Virginia Woolf.* In a long Introduction she examines these two strands in Woolf's non-fiction, but in contrast to Barrett, she is unwilling to see Woolf's materialist beliefs and her spiritual longings as irreconcilable. In an effort to elucidate Woolf's mysticism, Moore traces its connections with her feminism. In *A Room of One's Own* we can see that she perceived relationships between women in mystical terms, for at least ideally they are based on women's capacity for intuitive intimacy, for mutual knowledge based not on rational comprehension but on spiritual and sensuous friendship. In *Three Guineas*, says Moore, Woolf depicts powerfully and accurately the material bases of oppression and war, and these are in man's drive to dominate, in the system of property and in unreal loyalties, competitiveness and aggression. The question of how this catastrophic system could be replaced is answered in terms of a vision of womanly relationships and mystical values. It is, Moore says, the spirit of Antigone, not of Marx, that permeates *Three Guineas*. Woolf's political radicalism was based on a separatist vision not on her materialist insights. Woolf's feminist mysticism is to be found, moreover, in 'A Sketch of the Past', in which we can see a connection between images of mystical intuition and the infant's pre-Oedipal relation with its mother, which is experienced as a merging without boundaries. Woolf's highest and most urgently felt aspiration was to rediscover through her writing this state of infantile or mystical unity. The sexual equivalent of that experience was her homosexual passion for Vita Sackville-West, who provided for her a maternal protection. But more deeply, her desire was for creativity in solitude and a denial of the body.

Moore proceeds to a commentary on five of Woolf's novels within this framework of interpretation. She leaves out those novels in which Woolf's critique of society is most prominent, *Jacob's Room*, *Mrs Dalloway*, and *The Years*. Her treatment of Woolf is extremely unusual, for she takes *Orlando* to be her central work, her most extensive attempt to reconcile her materialism and her mysticism. It is in this novel that the basic theme of her life, her spiritual lesbianism, is most openly celebrated.

One way of assessing the influence of Woolf as one of the founding mothers of modern feminist thought is to look at the anthology of feminist literary theory edited by Mary Eagleton (1986). In this book Woolf is to be seen in the company of her many 'daughters' and it is notable that extracts from Woolf and Woolfian themes are to be found in every section of the book. The editor's introductions provide a useful short summary of the present state of the debate on many of the topics which Woolf placed on the agenda, on the history of the women's literary tradition, on the obstacles and constraints which stand in the way of women's aspirations to write and on the claim that there is a 'feminine sentence'.

I think it would be fair to say that whereas *A Room of One's Own* has had many champions and that it has had a profound and lasting effect on feminist literary studies, Woolf's other major feminist polemic, *Three Guineas* was far less successful. Although the questions it raised about the social psychology of gender and the social and cultural effects of gender divisions are still very much on the agenda, the positions which Woolf adopted in that work have not won so many adherents. Her conceptualization of patriarchy as a form of dictatorship, even a form of fascism, has perhaps been so disliked that other, more plausible, aspects of her argument, such as the connections between private property and militarism, and the infantile motivations which lie behind patriarchal hierarchies, were not given much of a hearing. What the book deserves, but has not received, is a careful commentary, a detailed scrutiny of its arguments. Although there is much passing comment on the book in various contexts (especially in connection with *The Years*, the novel from which *Three Guineas* split off as a separate work), there is no extended study of it in which its different strands of argument are disentangled and carefully evaluated. Catherine Smith (1987) defends the idea that it is a great work by viewing it within the genre of prophecy, specifically within a tradition of women's prophetic writing with which Woolf had some acquaintance. Beverly Ann Schlack (1977) analyses its rhetorical strategy. Unlike the seductive postures of *A Room of One's Own*, *Three Guineas* is an overtly scornful book in which a deliberately hostile and blunt verbal manner allows Woolf to give vent to her personal bitterness. It is a tone of voice which is not likely to win over the unconverted. Madeline Hummel (1977) discusses the epistolary form of the book. Naomi Black (1983) documents Woolf's feminist political 'activism' and argues that *Three Guineas* has a revolutionary message. Jane Marcus (1988) discusses the book in connection with Woolf's views on the proper relations between art and propaganda. Herbert Marder's book (1968) contains a summary of Woolf's views on patriarchy and arguments for regarding *Three Guineas* as the worst of Woolf's books. Brenda Silver (1983) provides a useful discussion of Woolf's composition of *Three Guineas* and its reception.

Poststructuralist Perspectives

Makiko Minow-Pinkney's (1987) study of five of Woolf's novels is by far the most substantial poststructuralist study of her work. I introduce it under this heading for two reasons. First, its theoretical agenda and vocabulary are largely derived from the work of Derrida, Lacan and other players in the French poststructuralist first team, as its lengthy subtitle, 'The problem of the subject: Feminine writing in the major novels', clearly signals. Second, Minow-Pinkney's main postulates might almost be taken as a definition of a poststructuralist approach. They are a denial of the ultimate validity of fixed definitions or dichotomies (such as that between male and female), a rejection of 'realism', indeed a scepticism about any 'reality' independent from representation, and a rejection of the unity of the subject, i.e., a person is taken to be not a unified and self-controlled agency but a dispersed and shifting bundle of contrary impulses and discourses.

Minow-Pinkney is interested in Woolf's modernism, her departure from the previous narrative conventions of the novel, and her book aims to assess the technical or formal features of these five of her novels from the point of view of feminist poststructuralist positions. The novels which she does not analyse at length are *The Voyage Out, Night and Day, The Years* and *Between the Acts*; this latter is a surprising omission, for as is hinted at in the few pages devoted to it here, it seems on the face of it to be the novel in which Woolf's discourse was most explicitly aligned with poststructuralist thinking. The thesis of Minow-Pinkney's book is that 'Woolf's experimental novels can best be seen as a feminist subversion of the deepest formal principles – of the very definitions of narrative, writing, the subject – of a patriarchal social order.'

Her book opens with an account of her theoretical concepts. The journey on which she takes us, rapidly zigzagging through the works of such as Lacan, Kristeva, Cixous and Irigary, might cause the reader who is inexperienced at tramping these heights of poststructuralist speculation to suffer vertigo, for it is full of hair-raising logical shortcuts and amazing conceptual leaps. I can only sketch in a few of the argument's most important moves. She opens with an exposition of Woolf's defence of modernist fiction in her essays, and she correctly observes that in the early 1920s Woolf stressed her revolt against the conventions of Edwardian fiction on the basis of a realist argument. Those conventions were seen as restrictive because they forced one to leave out aspects of life, of reality, that seemed to her to be of the utmost importance. At the end of the 1920s her emphasis changed and her stance became explicitly feminist. Now she wanted not just to assert the rights of youth to rebel against their fathers, but to proclaim the necessity of women overthrowing the rules of men. Her search for new literary form emphasized symbolist modernism, or poetic prose, forms of writing that stress the aesthetic, even musical powers of language rather than its supposed powers of representation. Whether or not a close reading of the essays would support this interpretation, one can agree that Woolf's aesthetic innovations and her feminist convictions were increasingly explicitly interlinked.

In *A Room of One's Own* Woolf explored the question of what it is to write as a woman and she settled on two apparently contradictory ideas: first, she insisted on the need for the writer to be androgynous and to be unconscious, while writing, of her sex; second, she spoke of the necessity for women to invent a woman's sentence, to elaborate a form of writing that was suited to the woman's mind and experience. But these two demands are not after all in contradiction, argues Minow-Pinkney, because Woolf does not intend the idea of androgyny to suggest that the male and the female aspects of the mind should merge or unify in any way that would suppress the differences between them. She insists on difference, not identity. The writer needs to be unconscious of her sex not in order that the differences should vanish but in order that they should be expressed even more clearly. The writer's androgynous mind opens to the play of difference and does not issue a homogeneous, undifferentiated language. The woman is privileged to attain androgyny, it is argued, because, unlike men, who take up their places in the dominant patriarchal order without having to bother themselves to identify imaginatively with women, women are forced, in learning to speak, to submit to the male symbolic order. Women, then, are inherently split or, as it were, bilingual.

In spite of this assertion, it is also argued that we must be careful not to take differences, for example, between masculine and feminine uses of language, as deriving from any *essential* difference between men and women, and certainly not from differences that are biologically determined (though Irigary, with her inclination to define women in terms of the anatomy of their sexual parts, breaks ranks in this respect). Male and female are not fixed essences but culturally differentiated constructions. Moreover, the identities in terms of which the difference is nominated ('male' and 'female') must not be taken to be, even at any particular historical moment, fixed or definable entities. At the poles of the dichotomy we find not definable essences, but shifting, heterogeneous and internally complex plays of difference. The androgynous woman writer, therefore, is a radical force who not only calls upon the different male and female aspects of her personality, but also can playfully open up each of these items to expose their multiplicity.

There is one further main strand of conceptual elaboration in Minow-Pinkney's argument that I should mention and that is the theory, taken from Julia Kristeva, that we should see writing as a double signifying process which partakes of both the symbolic order (the order of language, thought, society) and of the semiotic (the realm of rhythmic, body energies and drives which precedes language in the infant's developmemt and is associated with the pre-Oedipal relation between infant and mother). Kristeva's argument associates the symbolic order with the father, the masculine and patriarchy, and the semiotic with the mother, the feminine. It is the repression or marginalization of 'woman' which makes language possible. In other words, the repression or marginalization in speech and writing of prelinguistic rhythms and energies is associated with the repression of women. This alignment, apart from seeming, to me at any rate, inherently implausible, seems perilously close to postulating an essential definition of the feminine, a move against which we have earlier been warned. Minow-Pinkney, while using Kristeva's theory, accepts that some criticisms of it are persuasive.

Toril Moi (1985) offers her version of Kristeva's argument, again in the context of an account of Woolf's theory of androgyny. The symbolic order, she says, is a regime that is disrupted whenever the unconscious breaks through in playfulness, psychosis or poetry, or other manifestations of the return of the marginalized and repressed. *'The symbolic order is a patriarchal order'*, Moi solemnly (i.e., in true patriarchal fashion) announces. If ever a discourse were 'masculine', assertively staking out a position, then that of Moi surely is (regardless of the gender of its author), for in it there is not the slightest hint of playfulness, irony or infantile babble. Like so much poststructuralist celebration of the 'feminine' in writing, this is performed in a po-faced and muscular manner. The only inducement for the reader to go along with the theory that the symbolic order is a patriarchal order is an appeal to authority (the name of its author, Julia Kristeva). The only appropriate response seems to me to be loud, disruptive laughter.

Clearly, this is not the place for a patient examination of the axioms of poststructuralist feminist theory, but let me sound just one note of materialist sceptical response. Can 'the symbolic order' truly be said to be 'patriarchal'? Is it really plausible to assert that whenever and wherever human beings have developed norms of rational enquiry – strategies through language for managing their practical relations with each other and with the world, by labelling conceptual dichotomies and distinctions, by formulating definitions, by regularizing procedures of argument – that this has always been in the interests of male power and has always and everywhere had the effect of reproducing and consolidating patriarchal social relations?

Kristeva's argument is relevant to a commentary on Woolf's feminist theories in that it claims to provide not only a sophisticated theory of androgyny, but also, on the same basis, a definition of 'feminine writing'. This is defined as the space in which can speak the repressed term, woman's desire, female *jouissance*, which is 'arousal without climax', says Gillian Beer (1979), claiming that this contrasts it with the male variety of orgasm. It is the disruption of the symbolic by the semiotic. Apparently it is not taken to be an embarrassment to the theory that the most notable exemplars of this 'feminine writing' are Mallarmé, Artaud and Joyce, who all happen to be men.

Clearly, I cannot do justice here to Kristeva's ideas about androgyny and feminine writing. The differences between her positions and those of Heilbrun and Bazin are noted by Minow-Pinkney and Moi. The main target that both of them aim at, however, is Elaine Showalter. In their critiques of Showalter, it is another strand of poststructuralist thinking that comes to the fore, namely its rejection of 'realism'. In her critique of Woolf's idea of androgyny, Showalter had remarked that Woolf used the idea as a way of evading writing about her own experience, so that she did not confront her own anger and resentment. Because of this Showalter is charged, most vehemently by Moi, with being a 'realist' or – this apparently comes to the same thing – with being a liberal or bourgeois humanist, and a liberal individualist. In making the assumption that good women's fiction should present truthful images of strong women with which the reader could identify, Showalter demonstrated that she has not grasped that Woolf radically undermined the notion of the unitary self, which is, claims Moi, 'the central concept of Western male humanism'. Whereas Showalter wants a literary text to yield up a truth, a perspective that discloses some aspect of the world to the reader, Woolf, according to the poststructuralists, practices a deconstructive form of writing. Her texts expose the ways in which language refuses to be pinned down to an essential meaning. For meaning is indeterminate, endlessly deferred (the vocabulary here is that of Jacques Derrida). Woolf's characters, instead of being defined and pinned down by an authoritative narrator as in a traditional novel, are presented from many points of view. This multiperspectivism is Woolf's way of rejecting the idea that a person has a definable, unitary identity. Moreover, her rhythmic, poetic prose and unconventional narrative strategies are all part of her attack on and deconstruction of the death-dealing rigidities of the symbolic order.

What is at issue here is the question of whether we should interpret Woolf's fiction in 'realist' or in 'metafictional' terms (i.e., should we see her novels primarily as attempts to disclose some truths about the world and about human experience, or are they rather reflections on language, meaning and the conventions of fiction?) Woolf's own comments on the matter, it seems to me, undeniably show that she did, rightly or wrongly, at least in part understand her own work, her innovations in form and indeed the whole modern movement in fiction, in realist terms. For Woolf 'realism' does not involve one in positing a unified subject – in fact the whole conflation of these two issues seems a mistake. Perhaps the clearest way to identify the difference between Woolf's own position and that of her post-structuralist critics is to think about a doctrine which Minow-Pinkney puts like this: 'Experience', she says, 'never comes into being without representation.' I believe that Woolf's own deepest views on the purposes of literature run strictly counter to this doctrine. There are any number of places where she expresses the idea that the point of literature is to find verbal forms for expressing those parts of experience which are, precisely, inarticulate, which are painful or ecstatic precisely because they are *without* representation. So much of our most important experience is non-verbal in form, whether it be non-verbalized subconscious obsessions, mental imagery, inarticulate taboos, visionary wonder or obscure daily labour. Of course the traditional 'realist' conventions of fiction are hopeless at providing verbal forms for much of this mental material, but the answer is not to deny the realist, truth-telling vocation of literature but precisely to create new forms of realism, new conventions, so that literature can expand its cognitive activity, can open up to representation what has previously been repressed or ignored. Woolf has many names for these areas that must be rescued for representation. They are the dark country of women's experience, the submerged caverns of the unconscious, the lives of the obscure, the truth of a woman's passions and her body, moments of being or revelation.

The most important test of whether poststructuralist feminist theory has anything to offer is whether anything is gained when it is brought to bear not on Woolf's theoretical works but on her novels. It is here that Minow-Pinkney's book has its great strengths, for her approach does bring into clear view themes and issues in the novels that have otherwise remained either hazy or ignored. She provides a serious and lengthy commentary on *Orlando*, a novel which many critics fail to take very seriously. Orlando is the precise personification of the model of androgyny favoured by these critics, for she or he asserts and embodies gender difference while at the same time transgressing and exploding it. Some of the gains of Minow-Pinkney's approach are most convincingly on view in her chapter on *To the Lighthouse*, for example, in her discussion of Mr and Mrs Ramsay. These characters are often taken to be crude sexual stereotypes, with the hyperlogical, irascible, thrusting bully Mr Ramsay contrasted with his saintly, self-sacrificing, all-mothering and enveloping wife. However, read more carefully we can see that Woolf has wittily written these characters in such a way as to highlight the differences between the male and the female while at the same time deconstructing this very dichotomy. For, among many other details, the logocentric male is a fantasist and the subservient female is domineering. The binary opposition is simultaneously constructed and internally undone. As this terminology signals, this is one of the points at which Derrida puts in an appearance in this book.

Perhaps the best chapter is that on *Jacob's Room*, for this is a novel with which many critics have felt uncomfortable, and it is often treated as an apprentice or transitional work. Minow-Pinkney highlights the many ways in which the novel dwells on and ruminates on the problem of knowing another person. The central character, Jacob Flanders, remains to the end a mystery. He is, in the language of Derrida, an infinitely deferable, indeterminate meaning. There is a permanent gap between the subject who writes and the object written about. Minow-Pinkney shows how 'the impossibility of reaching a final truth precipitates a suspicion of signification itself', and dissolves the complacent assumptions of Edwardian realism. The meta-linguistic theme of meaning and its lost origins is detected throughout the novel. Of course, there is a price to be paid for this emphasis, for if one concentrates on such universal, philosophical themes one is bound to be less patient of all the ways in which the novel deals in matters that are more historically, culturally and psychologically specific. Not to put too fine a point on it, if you see the 'overwhelming sadness' which infuses the narration as a Derridean 'nostalgia for the lost origin', you may fail to explore its more specific causes. Jacob is not only, like the rest of us, an ungraspable lost origin, he is also dead. Moreover, his death was specific; he died as a soldier in the First World War. The narrator, being a woman and an outsider, found Jacob unknowable not merely in some metaphysical sense but in a way that was connected with the specific forms of exclusion that had separated them during his life. Such facts are not ignored in Minow-Pinkney's commentary but they are subordinated to the more universal theme. The general suspicion of meaning in the novel is in part a response to that historical catastrophe, and this is the occasion which reveals the more general truth, that there is a frustration which derives from language as such. Like all readings which, armed in advance with theoretical weaponry, perceive novels as exemplifications or dramatizations of theoretical truth, this one is bound to suffer some impoverishment as the price it pays for its capacity to bring into focus themes that would otherwise remain ignored.

Another book which, like that by Minow-Pinkney, focuses on the constant entanglement in Woolf's work of questions about gender difference with questions about representation, of literary form, is that by Rachel Bowlby (1988). Bowlby is aware of the fact that providing for Woolf a single, summarizing interpretation would be both untrue to her texts as well as in blatant contradiction with the poststructuralist premises of her own thinking. The main theme of the book is that Woolf's texts cannot be pinned down by the categories of feminism, modernism or realism, for while each of these categories is pertinent, none is stable in her writing. Her work is interpreted rather in terms of her shifting formulations and allegiances. In the end, Woolf is as much and as little definable and knowable as Jacob Flanders or Clarissa Dalloway.

Another book which adopts a theoretical perspective derived from both psychoanalytic and poststructuralist theory is Margaret Homans' *Bearing the Word*. However, the version of psychoanalytic theory that she uses is not that of Lacan or Kristeva but that of Nancy Chodorow. As Homans explains in her opening chapter, 'Reproduction and Women's Place in Language', this perspective emphasizes the differences between boys and girls in their relation to their mothers. The daughter identifies with her mother and 'does not need a copula such as the phallus to make the connection' with her body as the son does. She does not have the incentive (the threat of castration) that the boy does to enter the symbolic order. Therefore, the pre-Oedipal attachment to the mother lasts much longer for the little girl, in fact, beyond her acquisition of language. Unlike Kristeva, Homans does not regard this persistence of the bond with the mother as dangerous or psychotic. It was very strong in Virginia Woolf, as her earliest memories, recorded in 'A Sketch of the Past', testify.

The daughter's special relation to her mother and to language is the theme of Homans' interpretation of *To the Lighthouse* in the 'Postscript' to her book. Mrs Ramsay is the personification of Victorian ideologies of motherhood and womanhood. What is it for the daughter of such a mother (as Virginia Woolf was) to become a writer? Does it require the death of the mother, of 'the angel in the house'? Homans argues that Mrs Ramsay is an ambiguous figure in the novel, both loved and feared by Lily Briscoe. With her daughter Cam (usually a neglected character in comment on *To the Lighthouse*) Mrs Ramsay establishes a link with her body, through a non-representational use of langauge, that survives her death.

Gender and Woolf's Novels

In this section I discuss two critics who examine not only Woolf's feminist polemical works but also her whole literary *oeuvre* and who take questions of gender to be of central and determining importance throughout her work. Herbert Marder's study of Woolf, *Feminism and Art* (1968) is the main early work written within this perspective. It was written at a time when the mainstream of commentary on Woolf still took her novels to be devoid of social criticism and ignored the relations between her fiction and her feminist pamphlets. Marder's work was important in insisting on the central place in all of her work of social comment and a feminist perspective. He provides a useful sketch of the historical context of her feminism in the growth of the women's movement and the struggle for women's suffrage, and also in the decline of the Victorian family, an institution that caused her great personal unhappiness. He sketches her theory of patriarchy and of androgyny, taking this latter to represent a convergence of her feminism and her mysticism. This historical and conceptual material is then brought to bear on a reading of her novels, which he sees as representations of processes of reconciliation of opposites, of which the figure of androgyny is a central metaphor. *Night and Day* tells a story of the discovery of unity within social life. *To the Lighthouse* follows the search for unity in the development of integrated personalities. *The Years* traces the development of unity as a mystical ideal. Marder perceives a progression in the novels from social to mystical ideas of reconciliation. His treatment of Woolf's novels is extremely unusual in that it takes *The Years* to be her most successful work, in which the visionary

elements are better integrated into her depiction of the broad
stream of life. The novel's success derives from the fact that
her feminist point of view has become dispassionate ('impersonal' as she would have said), for whereas *To the Lighthouse*
is an attack on the male sex, *The Years* is not. Marder's
interpretation of androgyny as a merging or unity of opposites is sharply at odds with the interpretation of the poststructuralist feminists which I have discussed above. For
them androgyny emphatically preserves *difference*. Moi rejects Marder's interpretation of Mrs Ramsay as an androgynous artist as 'trite and traditional'.

The book regarded by many as the best feminist general
introduction to Woolf's career is Phyllis Rose's *Woman of
Letters* (1978). In fact this book, which is subtitled 'A Life of
Virginia Woolf', might well have been discussed as biography
or psychobiography in an earlier section of this book, for
chapters on her life alternate with chapters on her novels.
Throughout, the guiding questions are about women and
their struggle to achieve identity. The novels are viewed
primarily as investigations into the processes whereby
women achieve selfhood and the obstacles which they face in
doing so. For what does it mean to be a woman? How, in a
male-dominated society, can a woman integrate all her
various desires, aspirations and needs? 'For a woman', Rose
says, 'these issues have a particular urgency, because our
cultural tradition has so long and so strenuously discouraged
in women a strong and assertive sense of self.'

The central proposition of Rose's book is that feminism was
the crux of Woolf's emotional and intellectual life. 'One of
[Woolf's] triumphs as a novelist is that she made this tenu-
ousness of self the basis of her artistic vision and of new
literary modes.' Rose rejects formalist and philosophical approaches to Woolf's novels, which analyse both the form and
the content of her novels primarily in terms of aesthetic or
philosophical issues, questions about art, about self and
other, time and memory, being and non-being, and so on. Her
novels, it is argued, are not philosophical meditations but are
explorations of gendered problems of identity, and especially
of problems of selfhood for women struggling with conflicts

Phyllis Rose

between autonomy and intimacy, creativity and motherhood, femininity and self-assertion, all themes which are found not only in her novels but throughout her *oeuvre*.

Rose's emphasis on gender and personality as dynamic processes of achievement lead her to focus more on some novels than on others. Her treatment of *Night and Day*, *Jacob's Room* and *Between the Acts* is cursory. Her analysis of the 1930s is perfunctory (her conclusions are exactly the opposite of those of Marder, for she has little interest in *The Years* but regards *Three Guineas* as Woolf's best work in this period). Her treatment of *The Waves* is impatient and superficial. Her best, most substantial, criticism is of *The Voyage Out*, *Mrs Dalloway* and *To the Lighthouse*. She brings clearly into view that in these novels sexual passion is presented as a dangerous and disintegrative force for women, and that frigidity is shown as acquiring a strategic value as an attempt to preserve a sense of self. *To the Lighthouse* depicts varieties of womanhood, demonstrating how one can be a woman without being like Mrs Ramsay, who is taken to be a dusty, out-of-date, self-sacrificing character to whom the artistic spinster Lily Briscoe offers an alternative and preferable model. On biographical issues Rose has some fresh insights. Instead of viewing Bloomsbury from the point of view of its contribution to culture and its intellectual influence on Woolf, she sees it as a misogynistic milieu in which patriarchal attitudes survive dressed up in Edwardian male homosexual costume. In this perspective Bloomsbury did not have much that was positive to offer to Woolf in her investigations into womanhood and its historical vicissitudes. On the Woolfs' marriage, Rose's opinion is in sharp disagreement with that of Roger Poole, for she regards the Woolfs as having achieved an intimacy which was non-threatening for Virginia.

In summary Rose's book is a very good example of how an interpretive framework can provide different perspectives and refreshing changes of emphasis while at the same time leading to the neglect of issues that other authors perceive as crucial. It is arguable that the overall picture of Virginia Woolf that we obtain from this account is unbalanced because

she is presented as so consumed with her struggle to integrate aspects of her private life – marriage, sexuality, memory, family, friendship, writing – that she had no interest in
other issues. For example, one could argue that Zwerdling
gives a more balanced sense of Woolf's engagement with
social criticism and politics. Rose ignores aspects of psychology that were central to Woolf's own sense of her literary
aims, such as her methods of representing the dark caverns
of subconscious experience, of memory and of mourning.
There are even aspects of feminism which are minimized in
Rose's account, for she pays little attention to the theory of
patriarchy. Spilka's critique (1980) of Rose's book suggests
that the problem arises precisely from taking feminism to be
the crux of her career. This is not because he wishes to deny
the importance of her feminism but because it may be a
mistake to take any single theme as the one guiding principle
behind all her work, for this is to be too reductive. She was a
divided person in whom different aspirations were never
resolved. There was, in particular, a division between her
militant feminism and her aim for impersonal, dispassionate
artistic work.

Women's Literary Traditions

Virginia Woolf wrote that women writers should learn to
think back through their mothers. Do we see her own work
from an interesting new angle, with different emphases, if
we see it not just within the tradition of English fiction but
more specifically of English women's fiction? What are the
gains of highlighting gender in literary history? An interesting example of the difference it can make when gender is
emphasized is the topic of writing and the city. The usual
emphasis would be not on gender but on the category of the
modern. The city is the privileged terrain of modern experience, of the modern sensibility, and in modern fiction one
would expect to see a development of forms of writing appropriate to the exploration of this experience. This we do indeed
find in writers from Baudelaire to Joyce and Eliot. Brad-

bury's 'The Cities of Modernism' (in Bradbury and McFarlane, 1976) for example, provides a typical account of modern
city consciousness with its instabilities and velocities, its
excitements and shocks. The walker in the crowded streets
of Paris, London or Dublin experiences historically new
forms of aloneness and of encounters with strangers. The city
provides an objective spatial framework for unpredictably
contingent collisions and intersections, as in both *Ulysses*
and *Mrs Dalloway* (Maria DiBattista, 1983). Virginia Woolf
appears as a key witness in the company of Eliot and Joyce
in Raymond Williams' study (1973) of the literature of the
modern city, with Orlando's exhilarating, fragmenting mo-
torcar drive down the Old Kent Road in London cited as a
fine representation of the historically new experience of
speed. In her novels Woolf typically associated the discontinuity or atomism of subjective life in the city with the
problem of identity, the fact that modern life makes each
individual's growth into a coherent and integrated individual
endlessly problematic. This theme is discussed at greater
length in relation to Woolf in Hawthorn's book (1975) on *Mrs
Dalloway*. He concentrates on the experience of being alone
in a crowded city street as a perfect symbol for the alienation
of modern life. Is Woolf's vision of London as bleak as that of
Eliot's Unreal City in *The Waste Land*? Hawthorn emphasizes their common feeling whereas Dorothy Brewster in her
Virginia Woolf's London focusses on the more positive aspects of her vision.

But what if we ask not about the modern experience but
about women's experience of the city? Susan Merrill Squier's
Women Writers and the City contains chapters on both European and American writers (including George Eliot, Virginia
Woolf, Rebecca West, Katherine Mansfield, Margaret At-
wood, Willa Cather and Adrienne Rich) which is very refreshing after so many articles on the city devoted to Joyce and
T.S. Eliot. As far as Woolf is concerned, Squier contributes a
chapter on *Night and Day* in which this novel's plot is
contrasted with that of the classic city novel, for example, by
Fielding. In the latter the city is the scene for a plot of
education and marriage which ends with a return to the

country. In the Woolf novel the city has many typically modern connotations, both positive and negative; it is both a bewildering maze but also the site of honest work, it can be disorienting and yet it escapes the smug respectability of the suburbs. In the character of Mary Datchet, Woolf has written the portrait of a modern city woman. She is at home in the city, alone with her work in her private space. City life opens up for her possibilities that were denied to the females of the classic city novel.

Squier has incorporated her essay on *Night and Day* into a full-scale study of Woolf and the city, her book *Virginia Woolf and London: The Sexual Politics of the City*. Both here and in Brewster (1959) we find evidence that Woolf thought about London in terms of the literary tradition, with many references in her essays and diary to London as the city of Chaucer, Defoe and Dickens, including her moving invocation of this community of writers in her response to the destruction of London in the blitz in 1940 ('all that completeness ravished and demolished' she wrote in her diary). Squier and Brewster both open with commentaries on Woolf's essays 'Street Music' and 'Street Haunting'. In her experience of the streets, argues Squier, Woolf suffered divided loyalty and a divided identity, torn between her sense of being an insider (her class and her wealth making the city safe and exciting for her) and an outsider (excluded, like the street people, from the institutions of male power). Squier's particular contribution is to focus on Woolf's experience of London as a woman in a city that embodied and symbolized in so many ways the patriarchal society. In its public monuments the city commemorates male military heroes, in its buildings and processions the city celebrates male power. Squier's thesis is that Woolf's early view of the city as male territory often hostile to women, later deepens to and comes to include an appreciation of the city's power to embody women's experience. Woolf rewrote the city, so that it expressed feminist narratives and values, as, for example, in the story of Judith Shakespeare in *A Room of One's Own*.

Squier provides here what is, to my knowledge, the only commentary on Woolf's fine series of essays, written in 1931-

2, *The London Scene*, arguing that the essays subvert the
complacent genre of urban travelogue by portraying the city
as the scene of class and gender conflicts. There are also
chapters on *Mrs Dalloway* (it is interesting to compare the
different emphases of this and Hawthorn's book), *Flush*,
Three Guineas and *The Years*. In this latter novel, she argues,
the struggle for sexual and professional equality is fought out
on the streets of London. In preparing the final version of
this novel, Woolf, at the last minute, cut out two very large
sections, each of which centres on women's experience of the
city and an implicit social critique. Squier's analysis focuses
on these deleted sections and shows that there is a pattern
to Woolf's revisions, for she rejects early versions, which
contain direct denunciation of social ills, in favour of a final
form in which they are treated more indirectly. The drafts of
The Years are read as containing an implicit vision of an
alternative city of the future in which female values predomi-
nate and the patriarchal city of the past lies like Ozymandias
in ruins in the dust.

Another example of the gains that can be won by emphasizing gender is Judy Little's *Comedy and the Woman Writer*,
a book which was inspired by Virginia Woolf's remark that
comedy written by women may be different from comedy
written by men, and which examines this idea in relation to
the fiction of Woolf herself and Muriel Spark. Woolf has been
presented before as within the tradition of English comic
fiction, from Sterne, Austen, Dickens and Meredith, notably
by DiBattista (1980), a study of five of Woolf's novels. DiBattista rejects the emphasis in Woolf studies on biographical
fables and wants to see Woolf's work not in the context of her
personal traumas and idiosyncrasies but in that of the literary tradition. The emphasis is on the question of narrative
voice and narrative authority in Woolf's novels, and the
central figure is that of the voice of 'Anon', the poet who
speaks for the community. Judy Little, in contrast, presents
Woolf's fiction as speaking not for 'the community' but for
women.

Little's book opens with the theory of comedy. On a standard view comedy is a festive form which provides a mockery

of established social conventions, concerned especially with liminal (threshold or borderline) areas and experiences in which prevailing norms and forms of identity are overturned. It is therefore the domain of the unruly and ungovernable. Traditionally, at the end of comedy the norms are reestablished and the liminal elements are reincorporated into society. Women's comedy, she argues, mocks very long-standing norms. Because, as Woolf said, what is important to a man may be trivial to a woman, and vice versa, there will be a difference in women's comedy in the areas of social life that are joyfully undermined. Women can use comedy to criticize male values, even those which are so deeply and unconsciously held that their subversion can be experienced as dangerous and threatening. Women may make fun of conventional gender roles, myths, identities and archetypes, as Woolf mocks the angel in the house and male military heroes. At the end of women's comedy there may not be a reinstatement of the old order, but rather the generation of new norms and new models. Little criticizes DiBattista who, because she misses gender differences of comic tradition, is essentially conservative in her reading of Woolf, emphasizing her benign aspects rather than her social criticism, her articulation of communal values rather than her 'impudent hostility' to questing male heroes.

Little's approach allows her to bring out the virtues of Woolf's often undervalued early novels, *The Voyage Out* and *Night and Day*. She is also interesting on Woolf's most obviously comic novel, *Orlando,* the 'comedy of androgyny' as DiBattista calls it, and that 'festive comedy' *Between the Acts*, in which the village ritual has lost its capacity to generate a reaffirmation of order and cannot induce regeneration in the war-threatened community. Perhaps her best chapter is that on *Jacob's Room*, which she analyses as an *anti-Bildungsroman* or parody biography. In this novel the narrator's liminal vantage point enables her to view the young men of the British ruling class with amused scepticism. The novel is contrasted with *Portrait of the Artist as a Young Man*. Jacob's experience is, unlike that of Stephen Dedalus, antivocational. His years as a young man do not culminate in an experience of mission and clarified identity. Jacob has no epiphany or revelation. He is not defiant and does not, unlike Dedalus, refuse to serve. As a consequence, instead of discovering a vocation of self-expression as an artist, he dies in the trenches in the Great War. Jacob's short life is a painful parody of youthful rebellion.

5

Philosophical Interpretations

The Existential Project

Philosophical interpretations of a novelist's *oeuvre* divert our attention away from what are taken to be the relatively superficial topics that we have seen to be the main interest in psychobiographical, contextual and feminist readings. Philosophers have wanted to believe that there is some more profound narrative, or stratum of being, beneath the layers of personality and emotion, relationship and social life. The novels turn out to be not about patriarchy or bereavement, not sexuality or memory, but about such topics as Being or Silence. Moreover, in postulating some such stratum or deeper narrative, philosophical interpretations tend to look to it as the principle of unity which underlies and makes coherent the whole variety and evolution of an author's work. Thus, in spite of appearances of division, contradiction, or simply variety of interest, the philosophical reading will show the great writer to have been engaged in a single life-long project or search, perhaps the search for transcendence or the project of freedom.

Jean Guiguet's *Virginia Woolf and her Works* was first published in French in 1962. Intellectually it is very much under the influence of the prevailing philosophical culture in France at that time, which was Sartre's existentialism. For many years Guiguet's book was the standard reference work on Woolf. At its heart is a Sartrean reading of *A Writer's*

Diary, the only part of Woolf's diary then available, through which Guiguet attempted to discover Woolf's existential project, or what he calls 'the core of her being'. It is assumed that there is, if only we can find it, some central intention which defines both the author's identity and the trajectory of the literary work. This single, central truth, since it underlies the whole life and work, will enable us to grasp the unity of the entire *oeuvre*, for in spite of its apparently endless variety, experimentation and change, there must be a single guiding thread of purpose. As Guiguet puts it, the 'profound springs and fundamental principles…ensure the unity of her technique through all its variations.'

This 'centre and core of her being', the innermost source of all her work, takes the form, Guiguet says, of a world-view, a background philosophy or framework of philosophical concepts. It is in terms of this philosophy that we will be able to define the author's intention or purpose. Guiguet is very much opposed to the methods of psychobiography on the grounds that such work only touches on the more superficial aspects of a writer's being. In the life of a writer it is not the self of everyday life or that involved in intimate private relationships that is of interest. The 'deep self', the 'only real self', is that which the writer reveals in and through his or her works. Guiguet pursues his search for this philosophical centre of Woolf's work in two very long chapters, based on reading *A Writer's Diary*, before he begins his commentary on any of her novels, and he returns to it again in a concluding chapter. The main threads of existential reflection which he finds in her work weave around the categories of self, life, art and the apprehension of reality. Woolf's writing was a kind of philosophical problem-solving in which she returned again and again to these themes, looking over and over again for forms or devices that would allow her to express her philosophical reflections.

Guiguet made a particular point of studying the genesis of her novels, of following the various changes and decisions whereby they evolved from initial conception through many stages of formal elaboration and invention to their published forms. We now have, of course, far more information than he had about these histories of composition. However, there was enough information in *A Writer's Diary*, especially about *The Waves*, for him to succeed in establishing the connection between the form of her novels and her purpose in writing them, the statement or reflection about self and reality that she aimed to make. There is a dialectic of form and content in which philosophical reflection and novelistic technique evolve together. He correctly points out that her puzzles about self and non-self, about sensation and object, about consciousness and the unconscious, about time and timeless duration, are not problems which arose from her reading of philosophy. It is not a matter of 'influences', but of writing as a confrontation with the most important existential limits of our being. Her quest for existential integrity led her to abandon the conventional form of fictional character, for people are not fixed essences with precise outlines and well-defined characteristics. She wanted to stress people's indeterminacy, their existential anguish and ever-present potential for change and renewal.

Guiguet's account of Woolf's work plays down or ignores all those more materialist aspects of it which have more recently been defined and praised, for example, by Michèle Barrett. It could be argued that the weakness of this style of interpretation, which seeks above all else to demonstrate the underlying consistency and unity of an author's work, is that it ignores the inconsistencies or contradictions in it, and in Woolf's case, the apparent tension between her materialist insights and her mystical aspirations. In Guiguet's view, Woolf's consistent position was identical with that of Sartre, that 'man is essentially a consciousness, i.e., a potential of relations, whose centre is everywhere and whose circumference is nowhere, and which creates itself at the same time as it creates the universe.' ('Everywhere and Nowhere' is the title of a work by Sartre's contemporary and friend Merleau-Ponty.) Her novels, he argues, are an attempt to capture our primary relation to Being, to preserve our preverbal apprehension of reality that, in life, is covered over by and betrayed by the 'sclerosis' of words. She aimed, for example, to get back to a sense of time and space before they are rigidly

defined in terms derived from the material and
e.

The Creative Consciousness

The most elaborate philosophical study of Woolf's work in
recent years has been Howard Harper's *Between Language
and Silence*. Harper shares the common philosophical view
that it is the business of art to coax into language the most
profound, but silent, level of our being, which he identifies as
'the creative experience' or 'the creative consciousness', by
which both world and person are brought into existence.
Writing is the trace or record of this experience. In the work
of fiction the creative consciousness realizes its own poten-
tialities in an ongoing process of discovery. There is a voyage
(and *The Voyage Out* is an archetypal narrative of such a
voyage) in which there evolves a language of symbols and
myths. There is a search for meaning, and an intention to
escape given, conventional meanings so as to arrive at an
experience in which consciousness confronts its own possibilities and limitations. This experience is ineffable and yet
the creative consciousness seeks a symbolic language in
which its search can be dramatized.

In Woolf's work, the search for transcendent meaning
becomes the great mythic theme, which is enacted in each of
her works. They exhibit a common pattern, a common movement from anxiety or entrapment to a transcendent moment
of freedom. Woolf undertakes over and over again in her work
to narrate the journey from sexual anxiety to artistic vision.
For example, in *The Voyage Out*, Rachel moves from sexual
ignorance and panic to a strange visionary death. In *Mrs
Dalloway*, Clarissa moves from life-denying frigidity to life-
enhancing defiance via her visionary and vicarious experience of death. *Between the Acts* opens with Isa sexually
anxious and frustrated and closes with a cosmic vision of
sexual consummation. Harper argues that although some
such pattern is repeated throughout Woolf's work, there is
nonetheless a detectable change or evolution in the course of

her career. Whereas in her early work the journey is confined to a level of personal anxiety, later she achieves greater detachment or impersonality and her work takes on an epic, or even a cosmic, dimension. From *The Waves* to *Between the Acts* the story becomes more and more comprehensive.

Harper provides a commentary for each of Woolf's nine novels (this is unusual, for most critics make some selection which reflects the bias of their interpretive framework). As one would expect from his philosophical interpretation, he pays most detailed attention to their beginnings and endings. In addition, he traces the development of Woolf's narrative technique. She does not use an omniscient narrator but develops the technique of narrating from multiple view-points. He shows the philosophical significance of her increasing ability to synthesize, through the narrative voice, an ever broader range of perspectives. This 'narrative consciousness' dramatizes the transcendence of the limitations of the individual life. In *To the Lighthouse*, the voyage to the lighthouse, and Lily's successful journey to the completion of her picture, are myths in which are expressed the effort of consciousness to transcend its limitations and to find in art a means of synthesis and hence overcoming. The endings of her novels are characterized by a culminating moment of vision but also by the confrontation with the ultimate antithesis of intentionality, the fact of mortality. Ending with the confrontation with death is certainly a repeated pattern in Woolf's fiction. Again, however, there is a development. In *Between the Acts*, Woolf depicted not merely individual mortality, but the whole sweep of history, from the primeval to the present, and the inevitable demise of this twilight culture in spite of all the efforts of the obsessed writer Miss La Trobe. Harper gives a detailed analysis of the puzzling final pages of this novel, in which Woolf achieves an epic and a cosmic perspective on the little human dramas of love and hate, and confronts the immovable dualities of male and female, subject and object, fact and vision.

Such a philosophical reading relentlessly points us toward the most abstract level of meaning in the novels and shows relatively little interest in what are, for others, the central themes. A book that is less consistently abstract and far less tightly organized is Harvena Richter's *Virginia Woolf: The Inward Voyage*. Richter also discovers a pattern repeated throughout Woolf's fiction, which is that Woolf simultaneously acknowledges and denies 'the abyss'. She also sees Woolf's 'impersonality' or 'anonymity', together with 'the fable of androgyny', as basic to Woolf's poetic attitude. However, it is perhaps not so much in these themes that the main interest of this book lies, but in its discussion of perception and feeling. Her chapters are organized not so much around themes in Woolf's fiction as around these themes in philosophical psychology. For example, she discusses Woolf's essay 'The Moment: Summer's Night', and shows how Woolf conceived of the moment not as an atom of experience but as an extremely complex phenomenon. At one and the same moment a person perceives, remembers, feels, thinks and experiences time. So much of Woolf's prose was designed to unpack the unsuspected complexity of momentary experience, what she called 'the knot of consciousness'. Much of Richter's book is taken up with her analysis of Woolf's work as a reflection on the modes of perception, on the different modes of time and on the multiplicity of self. Perhaps the most unusual aspect of the book, however, is her discussion of the psychology of feeling, a topic generally neglected by both psychologists and philosophers. Drawing on the work of Susanne Langer, Richter discusses the pictorial means of presenting emotion, which are: image, metaphor and symbol. These are subjective modes before they are literary techniques and they are, being very close to unconscious in meaning, scarcely susceptible to psychological analysis. Woolf was unusual in her understanding of these pictorial aspects of emotion. Richter's valuable and original insight is that the fact that so much of Woolf's work employs imagery and symbol is not a consequence of some vague lyrical impulse but a quite specific and precise means of investigating, analysing and representing the emotional life with great precision and accuracy. Richter demonstrates this with detailed analyses of images as the repository of feeling in *To the Lighthouse* and *The Waves*. This is one of the more original and fascinating of philosophical studies of Virginia Woolf.

Unlike Harper and Guiguet, Mark Hussey, in his *The Singing of the Real World: The Philosophy of Virginia Woolf's Fiction*, does not attempt to impose on, or discover in, her work a single continuous and coherent philosophical message. Rather, he attempts to detect her own philosophical vocabulary and anxieties, and to allow her own voice to come through. He does not trace a single theme or project, though he does identify certain constant concerns and questions throughout her work. As a consequence, his book, while it is less tightly organized around a single theme, seems more true to its subject. In common with Harper, Hussey does not claim that Woolf was working under the influence of or in the shadow of any particular philosophical master.

In contrast to the books of Harper and Guiguet, Hussey's chapters are organized by theme rather than being devoted serially to Woolf's different novels. Her most constant questions arose from the fact that she was always torn between her optimism, based on a conviction that there is order and meaning to life, and her despair at the apparent emptiness at the heart of life. In her novels the most constant reflection is on the nature of the self. She longs to dissolve the barriers between different selves or to use her writing as a way of identifying a layer of experience which is prior to self, more primordial than the divisions into self and other, consciousness and world. According to Hussey, her conception of human being was essentially religious and was based on a belief in the soul. He defines her position as a belief in 'the self, or soul, an "essence" apart from all identities (apparitions) that cannot issue in the world but that may survive even death'. For Woolf, our known identities, our multiple selves, are just so many 'apparitions', or appearances, which deflect our attention from the unseen, the undescribable and unnamed self at the core of our being. Woolf was fascinated by the idea of the world apprehended not by our superficial 'apparition' identities but by our central being: the triumph of her novels is the apprehension of the 'singing of the real world' which is won, if only fleetingly, for language.

In this discussion, and indeed throughout his book, Hussey emphasizes Woolf's belief in and quest for the *preverbal* in experience. This idea was a central one in French philosophy, especially that of Merleau-Ponty, in the 1950s and 1960s. In one of the most original sections of his book he scrutinizes the holograph draft of *To the Lighthouse* and discovers in it passages, later deleted, in which Woolf describes the function of art as a unification of subject and object that defeats death. In 'Time Passes', according to Hussey, art rescues the human being from the dark nothingness of amorphous nature. His interpretation of Woolf stresses, far more than most, the religious content and inspiration of her work.

Time, Repetition, Deconstruction

There are a number of other studies which take Woolf's work, or parts of it, to be the expression of philosophical themes or which see philosophical ideas as a significant part of her meaning. James Hafley (1963) provides the most extensive study of alleged Bergsonian content in her works. I have already discussed above Allen McLaurin's book (1973) which gives an exposition of the aesthetics of Woolf and Fry. The entire second half of this book is given over to a discussion of 'repetition' as an aesthetic principle in Woolf's work and in that of, among others, Lawrence, Kierkegaard and Bergson.

Repetition or recurrence, as a textual mechanism for the production of meaning, is the central concept of J. Hillis Miller's book (1982). His main concern is to distinguish different kinds of repetitions in literature and to ask how they are to be interpreted. He has one chapter on *Mrs Dalloway* and one on *Between the Acts*. The former, he concludes, is an 'undecidable' text, which means that several different and quite incompatible interpretations of it are all equally defensible. The most peculiar aspect of the novel, over which there has been much dispute, is the strange relationship between Clarissa Dalloway and Septimus Warren Smith. As E.M. Forster put it, what is the connection between the societified lady and the obscure maniac? They never meet and have no known connection with each other at all, yet they each comfort themselves chanting the very same words of Shakespeare, and Smith's suicide at the end of the book has a curiously strong effect on Mrs Dalloway. It is as if he is her double. Taking this in the context of the larger questions posed by the book, it could be, says Miller, that we should see this as pointing to a world of union in death, a transcendent world of reconciliation and preservation existing within some non-earthly kind of time. Alternatively, we might take this 'doubling' to be without significance, to be purely a product of the plotting devices of the text. The undecidability of this question is itself an important philosophical conclusion. His discussion of *Between the Acts* looks more broadly at human and literary history of forms of repetition. The mind makes sense of the past by its activity of organizing it into repetitive series or patterns. The novel indirectly reflects on the significance of the mind's activity in generating meaning in these ways.

Geoffrey Hartman's 'Virginia's Web' (1970) is also concerned with the problem of where meaning comes from. He finds that Woolf's novels themselves represent the generation of meaning by the imagination. This it does by filling gaps between the discrete facts of experience, by connecting up separate events into patterns or series. The mind projects meaning into the spaces, and thus weaves a web among the discontinuities. *To the Lighthouse* both portrays and criticizes the affirmative impulse that produces this activity of the mind. The artificial character of the patterns in the web is shown forth in *Mrs Dalloway*. In creating a fictional world in which people and events connect up with each other in meaningful ways, the writer is not engaged in 'realism', in imitating or copying some pre-existing real web, but is indulging and displaying the mind's 'voracious desire for continuity'. Art is 'interpolation rather than mimesis', and Woolf's art is so clear-minded that it allows the reader simultaneously to witness the affirmative impulse filling the gaps and to catch a glimpse of the silence and ruin of the disorder over which the web is woven.

Paul Ricoeur, who is a distinguished French philosopher, includes an analysis of *Mrs Dalloway* in his monumental three-volume study *Time and Narrative*. He shows how the novel elicits what he calls 'the fictive experience of time'. The reader's experience of time in actual life is different in certain crucial respects from the experience of time gained from the encounter with the fictional world. Ricoeur's project is to explore the significance of this difference and of the intersection of time experiences that can occur in reading narrative fiction. In relation to *Mrs Dalloway* it is again the strange doubling of Clarissa by Septimus Warren Smith, and the fact that Smith's death is oddly life-enhancing for Clarissa, that suggests to Ricoeur that the novel may be offering some view of time different from the clock time that rules our practical lives.

Gayatri Chakravorty Spivak's article (1987) on *To the Lighthouse* takes the structure of the book as a metaphor for various themes, some philosophical. The novel is divided into three parts, two long parts divided by a short part in the middle. In the spirit of Derrida, the article plays with various puns. The short section, 'Time Passes' is like a hinge around which the other two parts turn. The time period covered by this part in the fiction corresponds roughly (very roughly in fact) to the period 1894-1918 in Woolf's own life, a period when, for much of the time, she was 'unhinged'. This thought allows Spivak to bring into her reading various bits of biographical information, for example, that in 1899 Virginia Stephen, as she then was, wrote a diary and a series of essays and exercises into a notebook which she had made by gluing blank pages into a second-hand copy of Dr Isaac Watt's *Logick*. This fact we are invited to take as a metaphor for Woolf's rejection, or covering over, of reason. To continue with the series of puns and metaphors, we can take Part 2 of the novel to be the narration of the production of a discourse of madness. In this unhinged discourse there is a disarticulation and undermining of predication. In predication we have a structure, which is again reflected in the structure of the text, of a subject and a predicate connected in the middle by the little word 'is'. This, in the language of the logicians, is the copula. In Part 2 of *To the Lighthouse* there is an uncoupling, both a deconstruction of the copula and an end to copulation, for Mr and Mrs Ramsay are separated by the latter's death. We can see the first part of the novel as the language of marriage, of coupling, with Mrs Ramsay as the subject, and the third part as the language of art with Mrs Ramsay as the predicate (the painting is or aims to capture the essence of Mrs Ramsay). This project comes near to being undermined or unhinged by the second part. The superimposed grammatical and sexual allegories have led us to a third, the novel as an allegory of the precarious creative power of art's own copula, for has the novel not in its way engendered Mrs Ramsay?

6

Practical and Thematic Criticism

Practical Criticism

Hermione Lee's bare title, *The Novels of Virginia Woolf*, warns us that, unlike most of the authors discussed in this and in previous chapters, she does not have an overriding thesis about the central meaning of all Woolf's novels, nor a single theme unifying her discussion of them. Moreover, she aggressively rejects the option of approaching the novels by way of themes from Woolf's life or cultural context. 'This is not a book about Bloomsbury, lesbianism, madness or suicide', she announces, as if it were obvious that such topics would stand in the way of an appreciation of Woolf's fiction. She is not going to read the novels as the working out of philosophical doctrine or feminist politics. She is simply going to go through them, unencumbered by any theoretical or conceptual baggage, reading them one at a time and commenting as she goes along on whatever strikes her as noteworthy. This is practical criticism, the responses of an intelligent and sympathetic empiricist reader, perhaps the famous 'common reader' with whom Woolf herself identified. Neither at the end of the book nor anywhere else does she attempt to pull together what she has discovered about Woolf's purposes, the shape of her career, the pattern of underlying intentions or meanings that animate the fiction. Having commented on *Between the Acts* she simply stops, with no conclusion or summing up.

Such an approach, in spite of its deliberate conceptual impoverishment, does have its strengths, most notably in its attention to textual detail. Having no overarching agenda, she can afford to linger over details that please or puzzle her, highlighting particular metaphors or oddities of technique that might otherwise escape attention. She conveys a much greater sense of appreciation of the verbal texture of the novels than many other critics. For example, in her reading of *To the Lighthouse*, Lee points out many of the subtle means by which Woolf has managed to write what is both a realistic story of family life, which nevertheless also hovers continuously on the verge of becoming symbolic, or even turning into a fairy tale or a Christian allegory about the conquest of death. The novel sustains both realistic and symbolic levels of meaning through its profusion of figures of speech, a poetic web of houses, shapes and journeys, and through its carefully controlled tone of irony and mild satiric mockery, combined with a deeper seriousness of moral purpose. Woolf herself, like her characters, may seem at first glance to be merely occupied with the small scale concerns of family life, but in reality, at a deeper level, her mind never wavers in its attention to bigger things, personal responsibility in the face of mortality and the consolations of art. Over and over again she shows us her characters saying 'pass the salt' or discussing their love of coffee while all the time their minds are suffering the pressure of broader questions and deeper feelings. Thus, even the most banal remark can carry some weight of symbolic meaning. When Andrew says, 'It is almost too dark to see', he speaks both of the evening light but also he, or perhaps the narrator through him, anticipates his own death. When Mrs Ramsay says 'It is too short', she is referring both to the stocking that she is knitting and also to life. Hermione Lee is very good at dwelling on and exhibiting in detail many such examples of the commonplace becoming infused with enriched significance. She is much less good when it comes to generalizing about this or other techniques or their place in the literary history of modernism, i.e., when it comes to asking why a writer might choose to write in this way, what problems they might be trying to solve or what previously ignored aspects of experience they might be trying to articulate. Her notes on modernism, in her introduction, are the only attempt she makes to see the wood as well as the trees, to understand and assess the overall place of Woolf's work. She decides that Woolf is 'a remarkable, though not a major figure' in the modernist movement and that she is in the second rank of 20th-century novelists. But her remarks on literary history are so brief and vague that one would do much better to turn to Lodge or Friedman on this topic.

Mitchell Leaska's book (1977) is another which opens by announcing its impatience with current styles of Woolf criticism which, being heavy with speculations about philosophy, abstract topics such as the nature of time, or discussions of form or aesthetic doctrine, all move away from what is the central point of interest, namely people. Leaska wants to get back to a discussion of Woolf's novels from the point of view of what, in detail, they say or show about their characters and especially about their inner lives. In an earlier study (1970) of *To the Lighthouse* he had developed an intricate method for analysing in very fine detail Woolf's use of multiple points of view, and in this later book he puts these methods to work in the analysis of seven of Woolf's novels (omitting *Orlando* and *Between the Acts*).

Technical and Formal Analysis

Jane Wheare's interesting and unusual book, *Virginia Woolf: Dramatic Novelist*, focuses on those novels which in most accounts of Woolf's work are either seen as having a very minor place in her *oeuvre* or, quite commonly, are ignored altogether: namely, *The Voyage Out*, *Night and Day* and *The Years*. In these novels Woolf's experiments with unconventional form are at a minimum. It is only in these novels that she extensively uses dialogue, quoting her characters at length in direct speech, which is why Wheare refers to them as Woolf's 'dramatic' novels. In her more unconventional novels, Woolf either employs the technique of free indirect speech, in which, by avoiding direct quotation, the narrator can give the gist of the characters' thoughts and feelings, both verbal and non-verbal, or she invents, in *The Waves*, a form of artificial soliloquy. By contrast, in the dramatic novels, she trusts the conventional forms of realism and, says Wheare, she thereby encourages her readers to believe in her characters as real people. She exploits the illusions of realist fiction, allowing her characters to speak for themselves and only expressing her own ideas obliquely.

This she achieves by a technical feature of these novels that Wheare emphasizes throughout her argument, which is, that Woolf chooses to avoid overt narratorial commentary. More generally, Wheare's main theme is the care with which Woolf creates the illusion of authorial absence from her narratives. In many traditional novels the narrator tells the reader how to understand what is going on. The narrator judges the characters, provides explanations for their behaviour and presents the reader with all sorts of general moral and social 'truths' in the form of sententious utterances and gnomic generalizations. Thus the narrator's authority and judgement is explicit and conspicuous. Woolf, in contrast, never allows herself to speak through the narrator. In this she is following the example of non-partisan authors such as Jane Austen and Walter Scott rather than that of George Eliot or Charles Dickens, in whose novels there is a geat deal of position-taking. Woolf's narrators are 'impersonal'. They do not reveal any of their own opinions as to the meaning of what is going on. They are not ideologists or propogandists. They do not preach. They leave the reader free to make up his or her own mind about whom to trust and what to believe.

This description of her practice in these novels helps us to understand what Woolf meant when she wrote in her diary that 'one can't propogate at the same time as write fiction', and what she was getting at in her pronouncements on art and politics, for example, in 'The Leaning Tower'. It also clarifies her much debated remarks in *A Room of One's Own* to the effect that the writer must not allow her own grievances or anger to contaminate her characters' speech.

Because of the unobtrusiveness of the narrator, Wheare argues, the reader is all the more ready to identify sympathetically with the characters and to trust them as the dramatization of ideological or political issues. For example, precisely because the narrator does not attempt to bully the reader into seeing things in a feminist way, she will be more willing to accept the feminist message that is inscribed implicitly into the dramas of the characters' lives in *The Voyage Out* and *Night and Day*. The clearest case of Woolf making this choice is her rejection of the essay-fiction format of *The Pargiters*. Her first intentions for this book were to alternate fictional chapters with essays in which she would offer explicit historical and social analysis and feminist comment. When she abandoned *The Pargiters* she decided instead to split the project into two quite separate books: *The Years*, in which the characters' lives dramatize the historical changes which had affected women's lives in the period from 1880 to the 1930s, but without narratorial/authorial comment, and *Three Guineas*, in which the author's anger at the patriarchal oppression of women and her analysis of men's psychology of domination and militarism, were both explicitly presented in polemical fashion with no holds barred. Wheare's commentary on *The Years* is her most substantial and interesting application of her theory. She shows how Woolf's presentation of dialogue changed between the drafts of this novel and its final form. For example, in the draft versions of conversations between Sara/Elvira and Maggie about the suffragette Rose, Woolf puts into their mouths many of her own political arguments, those which she later presented directly in *Three Guineas*. In the published version the characters make no overt political statements. Their points of view are expressed indirectly through the repetition of suggestive imagery and dramatized situations. (It is worth comparing Wheare's analysis of these drafts with that of Squier, 1982 and 1985.)

In her concluding chapter, Wheare takes issue with the views of Showalter and Stubbs, which I have discussed in ch. 4 earlier. Showalter argued that Woolf was wrong to repress her anger, and that her choice of androgyny represented a flight from her own emotions. Wheare, however, sees this not as a flight but as a tactical choice, for the reader can be trusted to be more receptive if the author's ideas and emotions are not imposed by being dragged into the fiction where they have no place. Stubbs argued that Woolf had failed in her own aims as a writer. She had proclaimed the ideal of representing women not only, as in previous fiction, in relation to men, but also in relation to each other. Moreover, she demanded that the novel should take as its subject the 'accumulation of unrecorded life'. Her novels, according to Stubbs, achieved neither of these objectives. Wheare disagrees, for whatever may be the case in her more famous modernist novels, her more traditional 'dramatic' novels do indeed succeed in these aims. *The Voyage Out* is not only about Rachel falling in love with Hewet, but is also about her relationship with Helen Ambrose, and *The Years* is about the lives of obscure women. Toril Moi rejected Showalter's and Stubbs' claims because she rejected the realism which they had demanded as naive. In contrast, Wheare rejects their claims for the opposite reason, because she believes that Woolf did after all choose realism and that this was an effective choice, defensible in terms of an effective feminist political strategy.

Another recent book that discusses Woolf's fiction in relation to her technique is Stella McNichol's *Virginia Woolf and the Poetry of Fiction*. Her theme is that Woolf was 'a poet who used prose fiction as her medium'. She wants to get away from the prevailing view of Woolf as a psychological novelist or social critic and to emphasize instead that she was a mystical/poetic writer. Her aim is to analyse the specific means by which, in the different novels, Woolf gave to her prose its poetic quality. For example, *Jacob's Room* is a 'poetic narrative' in which disconnected episodes are unified poetically via an interweaving of images and motifs. In *Mrs Dalloway* the poetry takes the form rather of a rhythmic order. *The Waves* is 'a playpoem', and *Between the Acts* is 'pure poetry'. McNichol rather loftily dismisses everything else written on this subject as irrelevant to her purposes. She thereby misses out on many useful treatments of the idea of the 'poetic' in Woolf's fiction in, for example, Pamela Transue

(1986), Friedman (1976), Richter (1970), and Mepham
(1976). For example, in her rather plodding reading of *To the
Lighthouse* she concentrates on the familiar poetic imagery
and the density of meaning that it creates. She misses some
of the other, more unexpected and more exciting, ways in
which the prose in this novel is 'poetic', for it uses not only
imagery but also many other resources of poetry, alliteration
and other phonetic patterns, rhythmic and metrical effects,
even the layout of the words on the page (Mepham, 1976).
McNichol's book also lacks a substantial and detailed commentary on Woolf's own essays on the topic of poetic prose,
for example, 'Impassioned Prose', 'The Narrow Bridge of Art'
and 'Women and Fiction'.

Michael Rosenthal's book (1979) is another that rejects
biographical and psychological readings of Woolf in favour of
a reading based on the appreciation of novelistic form. Feminist interpretations are also rejected in no uncertain terms.
He dismisses the 'polemical grinder of the feminist movement' which makes Woolf's commitment to feminism the key
to her fiction. In his view 'to focus on her fiction through any
sort of politicised feminist lens is seriously to distort it.' For
Rosenthal, each of Woolf's novels was the outcome of the
search for a particular form, and compared with the drama
of this search the details of her personal life are of no interest.
Her novels lack narrative interest and have no overt social
and psychological concern. In his preliminary chapters
Rosenthal reiterates this formalist thesis, and in his chapters
on the particular novels he pays special attention to their
genesis and development, as these are recorded in her
diaries, in an effort to show that her impulse always derived
from form and not content. She was, he claims, absorbed
primarily in creating shapes, not in character, theme or
philosophy. His commentaries on the novels are not at all
points consistent with this thesis, which he often, and perhaps fortunately, seems to lose sight of once he is engaged
with the texts themselves.

Themes and Theses

There are a number of academic commentaries on Woolf's novels which seek to identify in them some prominent theme or some single underlying obsession. For example, Lucio Ruotolo entitles his book *The Interrupted Moment: A View of Virginia Woolf's Novels*, for he sees as common to all her fiction the central importance of moments of disorientation, disruption and random intrusion. In this she is at one with other authors of modern life who perceive its particular quality as the shock, the sudden experience of instabilty or confusion, by which reason is ungrounded and the mind made sceptical of its own created meanings. One is reminded of Marshall Berman's title, taken from Marx's characterization of modernity, *All That Is Solid Melts Into Air*. Woolf, Ruotolo says, was ambivalent about interruption. On the one hand she longed, particularly in her more mystical or creative moods, not to be interrupted, and yet on the other hand she appreciated the ways in which interruption can augment our comprehension of the world by loosening the hold upon our minds of habits of thought, of complacently trusted mental schemata. The outcome of this ambivalence in her work was, says Ruotolo, an urge to fall back on artistic strategies of closure, to adopt an aesthetic of wholeness. Her novels form an arena of struggle between her desire for security or order and her clear-sighted recognition of the need to resist closure. The test of such thematic readings of Woolf lies in the extent to which they open up unexpected and fresh perspectives on the texts, allowing us to see characters or situations from a new angle. Ruotolo's book certainly, at least at times, achieves this. For example, he construes characters such as Jacob Flanders, Mrs Ramsay or Bernard (in *The Waves*) as the advocates of closure and bad faith. In *To the Lighthouse* it is Lily and not Mrs Ramsay who is the heroine, for she declines Mrs Ramsay's conventional satisfaction with wholeness. In *The Waves* Bernard is not Woolf's spokesperson, as he is frequently taken to be, for it is Woolf herself, with her insistence on reopening the novel at the end, after Bernard's defiant speech, who resists the appeal of closure. It is as if art poses for the writer and the reader a series of temptations (consolation, nostalgia) and yet in the end, as at the end of *Between the Acts*, should, to be honest, leave us dispersed, without a centre. The only honest modern conclusion is inconclusiveness. Ruotolo sees in Woolf's resistence of the seductions of coherence, especially in her last two novels, an increasingly 'anarchist persuasion' (and this is another of his fresh and debatable insights) to connect her aesthetics of interruption with her rejection, not just of patriarchy, but of 'the validity of social structure itself'. This is an interpretation of Woolf which sees her at odds with Bloomsbury formalism and which identifies her political vision as more broad than feminist.

One of the most interesting of these 'thesis' books is James Naremore's *The World Without a Self*. This discusses six of her novels, leaving out *Night and Day*, *Jacob's Room* and *The Waves* and, unusually, giving most space to *The Voyage Out*. He rejects the two critical approaches most common at the time, that which took Woolf to be a psychological novelist and that which focused on questions of time. Instead, he emphasizes the extent to which her novels have a double nature, being both visionary and also erotic. It is this latter, what he calls the curiously sexual quality of her writing, that has been most neglected by other critics. He devotes a whole chapter to the analysis of the 'stream of consciousness' method, and this is one of the best discussions of this topic available. His main concern is to point out that Woolf's writing is often described as if it aimed only to record, through direct or indirect quotation, the content of her characters' subjective experience. This is the emphasis given by all those many critics who lazily quote over and over again those same passages from her essay 'Modern Fiction' in which she asserts that life is a 'luminous halo', and that the writer should record the stream of 'atoms' as they fall on the mind. In fact, as Naremore rightly points out, this passage is commonly misunderstood, for it is given by Woolf as a description of Joyce's method in *Ulysses*, not her own. Her own work aims, over and above this, to express something that is outside or beyond the minds of the characters. She was, he observes, seldom inclined merely to record 'atoms' as they fall. Her narrative method does not amount merely to the transcription of ego, either the characters' or her own, but aims to be the voice of 'everyone and no-one', which is to say that her motives are less psychological than metaphysical. In visionary moments the individual consciousness breaks down or breaks through into some form of collective consciousness in which the barriers between individuals become permeable, a situation of merging which can be described in either mystical or erotic terms.

The topic of collective consciousness is also discussed by McLaurin (1984), again in the context of a study of the 'stream of consciousness', both as a psychological phenomenon described by William James and as a range of literary techniques. In fiction we find descriptions of a sundering of the barriers and partitions between individuals' streams of subjective life. There was among writers a current of speculation about group feeling or consciousness or 'collective mental being'. McLaurin shows that Bloomsbury writers were aware of these debates and that Woolf read some of the relevant texts including, late in her life, Freud's *Group Psychology and the Analysis of the Ego*. Woolf's 'fantasy of the common mind' is also discussed in Sara Ruddick (1981) in a very fine article about *Jacob's Room*. Something of what this idea is about is suggested by a passage taken from Woolf's 1903 diary, which is quoted by Ruddick (p. 194): 'I think I see for a moment how our minds are all threaded together – how any live mind today is of the very same stuff as Plato's and Euripedes: It is only a continuation and development of the whole thing – it is this common mind that bends the whole world together and all the world is mind.'

Overcoming the barriers of individual consciousness is a main theme in Naremore's (1973) commentaries on the particular novels. These are also characterized by an unusually careful scrutiny of details of language, of Woolf's phrasing, narrative transitions and ambiguities of voice. There are many excellent and intriguing discoveries. His discussion is often in the line of critical inquiry opened up by Auerbach (1953), asking, beyond all the technical detail, 'What vision of life determines this style?' All of Woolf's innovations, experiments and technical peculiarities derive from an intensely serious search, the impulse behind all her work, for unity. As the title of *Between the Acts* suggests, that book is about unfilled spaces, and 'the great problem that animates this novel, as indeed all Mrs Woolf's novels, is whether to deny or accept the terrible sense of separation between things.' She wrote in order to investigate the varieties of ways in which the space between things could be overcome, in which people could be drawn into an *embrace*, whether in erotic experience, moments of vision or in death.

In addition to the books I have mentioned above, another useful resource are the various anthologies of essays on Woolf, of which there are now quite a number. Beja (1985) is useful because it reprints chapters from some of the books above (including Hillis Miller, Heilbrun, Naremore, Marcus, Rose, Rosenthal, Richter and Squier) as well as some others that are worth reading, notably Fleishman (1975) and, Joanne Trautmann (1973). Other anthologies that could be consulted, in addition to those edited by Jane Marcus, which I have mentioned in other contexts, are Warner (1984), Clements and Grundy (1983), Sprague (1971), Freedman (1980) and Ginsberg and Gottlieb (1983).

I had a little tool shed,
where the children bled,
it made them sad and it made me glad
My sweet Satan!,
sweet sweet Satan

7

Editions, Drafts and Agendas

In this chapter I will give information about the many published drafts of Woolf's novels. I do this because so much
commentary on her work has dwelt on the genesis and
evolution of her novels. Choices that she made in the course
of writing them are sometimes very revealing as to her state
of mind, her artistic intentions or the technical difficulties
she faced in bringing her more experimental works to conclusion. In fact, it is striking how often formal aspects of her
novels, which are crucial to their meaning in the final versions, were only introduced at a very late stage in the process
of composition. In addition, I will also give here an indication
of some of the main areas of debate in relation to each of her
works and some of the more specialist discussions of them.
But I must stress that the debates mentioned in this chapter
are in addition to the main critical work on the novels, which
is to be found in the books covered in earlier chapters and
which I will not usually refer to again here.

The standard edition of Woolf's novels is the Uniform
Edition, published by the Hogarth Press in Britain (and by
Harcourt Brace Jovanovich in the USA) starting in 1929.
Woolf sometimes corrected proofs of the British and American editions separately and there are, to this day, curious
differences between them which unwary teachers travelling
across the Atlantic sometimes stumble upon. Modern paper-
back editions have been printed using those Uniform Edition
versions without revision. Now that in 1992, in Britain, the

novels have come out of copyright, popular editions are proliferating and scholarly editions are in preparation.

The Early Novels

The Voyage Out started life as a novel called *Melymbrosia* and it underwent many years of writing and rewriting before eventually being published in 1915. Many draft versions exist. *Melymbrosia: An Early Version of The Voyage Out* (1982) was edited by Louise DeSalvo who has also written a detailed study of other extant drafts and proofs of the novel, *Virginia Woolf's First Voyage: A Novel in the Making* (1980). *Night and Day* is one of the least highly regarded of Woolf's novels. Many critics have found it tedious, but fortunately, in recent years it has found its defenders, and there are particularly good disussions of it in Squier (1985) and Marcus (1988).

Modernist Novels

The draft versions of *Jacob's Room* have not excited scholars as much as many of the other novels. E.L. Bishop (1986) discusses Woolf's manuscript revisions. The most puzzling feature of the novel is the narrator who, uniquely in Woolf's novels, is a 'personal' narrator, using the first person to address the reader. At the same time there seems to be a more conventional, omniscient third-person narrator at work. This puzzling structural aspect of the novel is discussed by Barry Morgenstern (1972). Karen Lawrence (1986) compares the narrators in *Jacob's Room* and *Portrait of the Artist as a Young Man*. Judy Little (1983) discusses the novel as a parody biography or as an *anti-Bildungsroman* and Sara Ruddick (1981) has many interesting things to say about the character of Jacob Flanders from a feminist point of view.

Virginia Woolf herself published in 1928 an account of the development of the main features of *Mrs Dalloway* (this was the only one of her novels for which she did this). The manuscript revisions are discussed in Hoffmann (1968) and Latham (1972). Woolf originally set out to write a collection of stories and these were, in the event, only finished later and only published as a collection, *Mrs Dalloway's Party*, in 1973. Stella McNichol's introduction to that volume gives a sketch of this history. I have already mentioned earlier the main areas of debate in relation to *Mrs Dalloway*. Marxists have raised the question of the extent to which the limitations of its criticism of the social system are symptomatic of a general problem in Woolf's art, which derives from her class position. John Hillis Miller (1982) discusses the significance of the 'doubling' of Clarissa Dalloway and Septimus Warren Smith, which may or may not indicate some belief in a transcendent realm of common experience. Ricoeur (1985) discusses the treatment of time in the novel. The most extensive study of Woolf's innovations in the literary creation of character is in Baruch Hochman (1983), which focuses on *Mrs Dalloway*. A very useful collection of articles on *Mrs Dalloway*, which will focus on rather different topics, and will include writing by Hillis Miller, Minow-Pinkney, Bowlby and others, will be the forthcoming 'New Casebook' edited by Su Reid.

Susan Dick (1983) has edited the holograph draft of *To the Lighthouse*. This, apart from being a marvel as a printed book, for it reproduces in inventive notations all of Woolf's deletion marks, rewritings, marginalia, and so on, is also an extremely interesting source for anyone wishing to try to follow her creative process. One can witness the finished version of the book emerge out of much slacker and more hesitant earlier versions. It provides very clear examples of how, when writing, Woolf was searching for a rhythm and would hesitate and rewrite a passage over and over again until the right rhythmic sentence began to flow freely. We can see too, what a very large amount of tightening up she would do at the last stage, pulling the whole text together by carefully selecting images, and throwing out anything that spoiled the very beautifully controlled pace of the writing. This book also contains other relevant material from Woolf's notebooks and a detailed introduction by Susan Dick.

Mitchell Leaska (1970) wrote a detailed analysis of *To the Lighthouse*, concentrating on an attempt to specify very precisely just what is involved in Woolf's narrative methods, her use of multiple points of view and her poetic prose, involving dense, highly controlled imagery. Morris Beja (1970) edited a 'Casebook', which collects together both early reviews of *To the Lighthouse* and also subsequent criticism, including extracts from sources I have mentioned such as Guiguet, Hafley and Auerbach. Mepham (1976) gives an analysis of the poetics of *To the Lighthouse*, and parts of this, together with extracts from books by Abel, Lodge and other recent discussions, are to be included in Su Reid's 'New Casebook'. This volume seems likely to be the best place to find out about the agenda in current discussion of this novel. Su Reid has also written (1991) a short survey of the critical debates about *To the Lighthouse*, in which the various contributions are classified into the different styles of critical argument, feminist, structuralist, New Criticism, Freudian, and so on.

Madeline Moore (1979) has edited and introduced a manuscript draft of *Orlando* and appended to it a selection of relevant letters from Woolf, Vita Sackville-West and Harold Nicolson. The Sackville-West/Woolf letters have been edited by DeSalvo and Leaska (1984). The biographical background to the book in the relationship between these two women has been much studied; see, for example, Joanne Trautmann (1973) and Frank Baldanza (1955). Critics are divided on how seriously to take *Orlando*. Woolf herself was worried that it might fall between two stools, being too long for a joke and too lightweight as a serious novel. Hermione Lee's commentary (1977) is good on the unevenness of tone which makes it less satisfactory towards the end. More admiring comment on the novel can be found in J.J. Wilson, 'Why is *Orlando* Difficult?' (1981): her answer is that it is in the tradition of the anti-novel. See also John Graham, 'The "Caricature Value" of Parody and Fantasy in *Orlando*' (1971), and chapters in Moore (1984) and Minow-Pinkney (1987).

John Graham has transcribed and edited two holograph drafts of *The Waves* (1976) and this book is another wonderful example of inventive printing. The text is so laid out that one can see at a glance all of Woolf's deletions and emendations and can appreciate the speed of her writing. Sometimes she is hesitant and goes slowly back over the same phrasing again and again, at other times, particularly towards the end, her pen travelled across the page almost in a trance of inspiration. These manuscripts are among those which demonstrate that some of her most remarkable formal devices, such as in this case the use of italicized 'interchapters', were only introduced at the final stages of composition. There is a large amount of information about the evolving conception and composition of this book in Woolf's diaries, perhaps easiest read in *A Writer's Diary*. Critical comment on the novel, the most difficult and abstract of all Woolf's novels, can be found throughout the secondary literature which I have mentioned above. Eric Warner (1987) has written a whole book devoted entirely to *The Waves* and this is a good starting point for a study of the critical debate. I should also mention here *Women and Fiction: The Manuscript Versions of A Room of One's Own*, edited by S.P. Rosenbaum (1992).

The 1930s

Flush is a minor piece of work, a fictional biography of a dog, and there is not much critical comment on it. Szladits (1970) offers an appreciative essay. Trombley (1981) has a provocative hypothesis as to its hidden source in Woolf's emotional life. Squier (1985) has an interesting discussion of it in her study of Woolf and London. McLaurin (1973) discusses the novel in relation to a serious and puzzling question in aesthetic theory, which had been raised by Roger Fry, namely whether there could be an art based on the sense of smell, the problem arising from the fact that smells are not amenable to the establishment of complex relations, only lists and connotations.

No novel since *The Voyage Out* cost Woolf so many years of agonized indecision and uncertainty as *The Years*. It began as *The Pargiters*, a highly original work in which fictional chapters alternated with essays, the whole being an attempt to investigate and dramatize the situation of women in the family and society from the late Victorian period through to modern times. The draft of this book has been published (1978) and it is fascinating to speculate just what might have come of this project had she not abandoned it. This same volume, edited by Leaska, also contains the typescript of a speech that Woolf gave to a women's society in 1931, which is, in effect, a much longer and very interesting version of her essay later published as 'Professions for Women'. It is here that she reveals her famous thoughts on the necessity of killing the angel in the house. Her project changed and became the novel *The Years*. When she finally produced a finished version of this it was some 200,000 words in length. Woolf panicked, being very unsure of its quality. She cut out a large amount of material at this stage, including two very long sections which have been subsequently printed and much commented upon. They are included in Grace Radin (1981) together with a detailed commentary on this draft and other early versions of the novel. Other very interesting bits of typescript draft are printed in Squier (1982). Again one can speculate what the novel would have been like had she not made this dramatic choice, and these sources allow one to appreciate in detail just what kind of changes in her conception of the novel Woolf made as it evolved. The significance of these changes is analysed also in Wheare (1989).

The Years, though popular in terms of sales, was not highly regarded by critics. Transue (1986) has a good chapter on *The Years*, with a summary of different critical assessments of it. Until recently it was almost universally rejected as a failure. Now, however, a vigorous defence of the book's merits has been mounted, not least by Jane Marcus who claims that this novel is a female epic, Woolf's answer to *Ulysses*. It is, she says, a great novel, 'the pride of British literature of the 1930s'. This article, together with many others on this novel can all be found in a special issue of the *Bulletin of the New York Public Library* (1977) devoted to *The Years* and *Three Guineas*. Other useful critical comment can be found in Gottlieb (1983) and Schaefer (1971). I have not been able to examine what promises to be a very useful collection of articles of relevance here, *Virginia Woolf and War: Fiction, Reality and Myth*, edited by Mark Hussey (1992).

Woolf's last novel, which she had not finished revising at the time of her death, was *Between the Acts*, of which the original title was *Pointz Hall*. Leaska (1983) has edited two typescript versions of the novel and this book also contains a very thorough discussion of its evolution by the editor. When she died Woolf also left manuscripts of other unfinished work, the most important of which was a projected book on the history of English literature, bits of which were published as 'Anon' and 'The Reader' in 1979, edited by Brenda Silver. Nora Eisenberg (1981) sees 'Anon' and *Between the Acts* as sharing a theme, a utopian old world in which communal life flourished, free from male domination. Both works also celebrate the overcoming of male conventional language by a communal, little language of song, dance and gesture.

Other Writings

Virginia Woolf published only one collection of stories in her lifetime, *Monday or Tuesday*, in 1921. These and all of her other stories are now available in *Virginia Woolf: The Complete Shorter Fiction*, edited by Susan Dick. Some of the stories, especially 'The Journal of Mistress Joan Martyn', 'The Mark on the Wall', and 'Kew Gardens', were important early experiments in fictional ideas and form, written before Woolf had published a modernist novel. As such, these stories often appear in accounts of Woolf's early career. Stories in the *Mrs Dalloway's Party* sequence had a part in the history of *Mrs Dalloway*. Critical comment upon Woolf's stories in their own right is scarce, though there are essays by Fleishman and Hafley in the volume edited by Freedman (1980). Selma Meyerowitz (1981) argues that though most critics have read Woolf's stories as lyrical and metaphysical experiments, they can, in fact, be read in terms of her political vision and her critique of society. They are about class and alienation and women are portrayed as outsiders for whom personal relationships are painful and unfulfilling.

As a young writer at the beginning of her career – for ten years before publishing her first novel – Virginia Woolf wrote hundreds of reviews and essays, many of which, having been published anonymously, are only now coming to light. She continued to be a prolific essayist throughout her career. There have been a confusing number of collections and editions of her essays over the years. In her lifetime she published two volumes, *The Common Reader: First Series* (1925) and *The Common Reader: Second Series* (1932). After her death Leonard Woolf edited and published *The Death of the Moth* (1942), *The Moment and Other Essays* (1947), *The Captain's Deathbed* (1950) and *Granite and Rainbow* (1958). He then collected all these essays into the four volumes of *Collected Essays* (1966). These volumes do not, by a long way, contain all of his wife's essays. Moreover, they are very uninformative about the dates of composition and publication of many of the essays and he provided no notes on his wife's sources and no index. Yet further collections were published later, such as *Contemporary Writers* (1965), edited by Jean Guiguet and *Women and Writing* (1979), introduced by Michèle Barrett. Fortunately, a complete edition, *The Essays of Virginia Woolf*, meticulously edited by Andrew McNeillie, with a wealth of annotation and editorial information, and containing many essays which have not been reprinted since their original appearance in newspapers and magazines, is now in the process of publication.

Perhaps the most original study of Woolf's essays is by Perry Meisel (1980). He argues that Woolf's ideas on aesthetics (as well as her novels) were influenced by Walter Pater, though this influence caused her anxiety and is carefully made invisible. (The 'anxiety of influence' model is derived from the work of Harold Bloom). There is no discussion of Pater in her work, but Meisel traces in her essays many of Pater's habits of thought and vocabulary, for example his celebration of personality and of the privileged moment, and his 'chemical vocabulary' for the artist's 'crystalline or incandescent expressiveness'.

Bell and Ohmann (1975) put forward a convincing argument about the merits of Woolf's style as an essayist. They claim that her critical writing was feminine in tone and was in revolt against the male conventions of the form. She rejected systematic thinking in her essays and had no interest in battles between different critical schools of thought. She chose instead an impressionistic style which, they argue, was truly revolutionary in its address to the reader, its amiable tone, its unpretentious, non-authoritarian, modest stance. She adopts the persona of 'the common reader' and appeals to other common readers through her exceptionally clear and vivid prose. Her status as an outsider allowed her a liberated viewpoint, and in consequence she was able to write regularly about books that were outside the accepted canon of English literature. She was 'unprofessional' in all the very best senses of that word.

Mark Goldman (1976), in the only book-length study of her essays to date, argues that Woolf's status as an essayist is still uncertain. He provides a useful review of earlier comment on her essays, noting that she has often been dismissed as a charming but impressionistic and subjective essayist. In his view, a unity of critical thinking, an overall coherence, can be discerned in her work. Her essays are best seen as being by an artist-critic who looks at writing from the point of view of a practising writer.

Woolf wrote a biography of her friend Roger Fry and several essays on the subject of biography. Phyllis Rose in *Writing of Women* has an excellent discussion, in which Woolf is a central point of reference, of problems of biography, and especially problems with writing women's lives. Michael Holroyd (1976), himself a literary biographer, comments on the weaknesses of *Roger Fry* and the difficulties that Woolf had in writing it. He also criticizes Quentin Bell's biography of Woolf and discusses the question of why she is such a very difficult subject for the biographer. Thomas Lewis (1983) compares her fictional with her non-fictional biographies.

A great deal of use has been made of Woolf's autobiographical writings, published as *Moments of Being*, in the biographical and psychobiographical works discussed above.

There has not been so much comment on the literary form and value of this work. Griffin (1981) assesses the pieces in this book as autobiography. Mepham (1991) compares and contrasts *Roger Fry* and 'A Sketch of the Past', which were written at roughly the same time, arguing that Woolf was provoked by writing the biography into a profound reflection upon the forms of 'life-writing' and that 'A Sketch of the Past', which was the result, is one of her finest works. Lyndall Gordon (1983) discusses Woolf's views on, and her practice of, biography and autobiography, and shows the connections with her notion of 'moments of being'. She compares Woolf's views with those of T.S. Eliot.

There is a certain amount of serious literary criticism, as distinct from biographical or historical reaction, of Woolf's letters and diary. Phyllis Rose (1985) and Mepham (1980) discuss the letters. Blanchot (1982) reacts to *A Writer's Diary* by celebrating Virginia Woolf's dedication to her vocation as a writer.

Bibliography

(cross references are marked *)

Works by Virginia Woolf

Main Published Works

(Listed in chronological order, with dates of first publication. The Uniform Edition of the Works of Virginia Woolf is published in the UK by the Hogarth Press and in the USA by Harcourt Brace Jovanovich.)

The Voyage Out (1915)
Night and Day (1919)
Monday or Tuesday (1921)
Jacob's Room (1922)
Mrs Dalloway (1925)
The Common Reader: First Series (1925)
To the Lighthouse (1927)
Orlando (1928)
A Room of One's Own (1929)
The Waves (1931)
The Common Reader: Second Series (1932)
Flush: A Biography (1933)
The Years (1937)
Three Guineas (1938)
Roger Fry (1940)
Between the Acts (1941)

Other Works by Virginia Woolf

A Cockney's Farming Experience, (ed.) S. Henig (San Diego State University Press, 1972)

'Anon' and 'The Reader', *Twentieth Century Literature* 25 (1979), pp. 356-435

Collected Essays, vols 1-4, (ed.) Leonard Woolf (Chatto & Windus, 1966)

The Complete Shorter Fiction, (ed.) Susan Dick (Hogarth, 1985)

The Diary of Virginia Woolf: Volume I: 1915-1919, Volume II: 1920-1924, Volume III: 1925-1930, Volume IV: 1931-1935, Volume V: 1936-1941, (ed.) Anne Olivier Bell assisted by Andrew McNeillie (Hogarth, 1977-84)

The Essays of Virginia Woolf: Volume I: 1904-1912, Volume II: 1912-1918, Volume III: 1919-1924, (ed.) Andrew McNeillie (Hogarth, 1986-88)

The Letters of Virginia Woolf: Volume I: 1888-1912, Volume II: 1912-1922, Volume III: 1923-1928, Volume IV: 1929-1931, Volume V: 1932-1935, Volume VI: 1936-1941, (ed.) Nigel Nicolson and Joanne Trautman (Hogarth, 1975-80)

The London Scene: Five Essays (Hogarth, 1982)

Melymbrosia: An Early Version of 'The Voyage Out', (ed.) Louise DeSalvo (New York Public Library, 1982)

Moments of Being: Unpublished Autobiographical Writings, (ed.) Jeanne Schulkind (Chatto & Windus for Sussex University Press, 1976; 2nd edn, 1985)

Mrs Dalloway, Introduction by Virginia Woolf (Modern Library, Random House,1928)

Mrs Dalloway's Party: A Short Story Sequence, (ed.) Stella McNichol (Hogarth, 1973)

The Pargiters: The Novel–Essay Portion of The Years, (ed.) Mitchell Leaska (Hogarth, 1978)

A Passionate Apprentice: The Early Journals, 1897-1909, (ed.) Mitchell Leaska (Hogarth, 1990)

Pointz Hall: The Earlier and Later Typescripts of Between the Acts, (ed.) Mitchell Leaska (New York University Press, 1983)

'A Terrible Tragedy in a Duckpond', *Independent on Sunday Magazine* (8 April 1990); also in **A Passionate Apprentice*

'To the Lighthouse': *The Original Holograph Draft*, (ed.) Susan Dick (Hogarth, 1983)

'The Waves': *The Two Holograph Drafts*, (ed.) J.W. Graham (Hogarth, 1976)

Women and Fiction: The Manuscript Versions of A Room of One's Own, (ed.) S.P. Rosenbaum (Blackwell, 1992)

Women and Writing, Introduced by Michèle Barrett, (The Women's Press, 1979)

A Writer's Diary, ed. Leonard Woolf (Hogarth, 1953)

Secondary Works

Abel, E., *Virginia Woolf and the Fictions of Psychoanalysis* (University of Chicago Press, 1989)

———— ' "Cam the Wicked": Woolf's Portrait of the Artist as her Father's Daughter' in *(ed.) Su Reid, *New Casebook*

Ackroyd, P., *T.S.Eliot* (Hamish Hamilton, 1984)

Annan, N., *Leslie Stephen: The Godless Victorian* (University of Chicago Press, 1986)

———— 'Bloomsbury and the Leavises' in *(ed.) J. Marcus, 1987

Ascher, C., DeSalvo, L., and Ruddick, S., *Between Women: Biographers, Novelists, Critics, Teachers and Artists Write about Their Work on Women* (Beacon Press, 1984)

Auerbach, E., *Mimesis: The Representation of Reality in Western Literature* (Princeton University Press, 1953)

Baldanza, F., 'Orlando and the Sackvilles', *Proceedings of the Modern Languages Association of America* 70 (1955), pp. 274-9

Barrett, M., 'Introduction' to Virginia Woolf, *Women and Writing* (The Women's Press, 1979)

Bazin, N.T., *Virginia Woolf and the Androgynous Vision* (Rutgers University Press, 1973)

Beer, G., 'Beyond Determinism: George Eliot and Virginia Woolf' in (ed.) Mary Jacobus, *Women Writing and Writing About Women* (Croom Helm, 1979)

Beja, M. (ed.), *Virginia Woolf: 'To the Lighthouse': A Casebook* (Macmillan,1970)

———— *Epiphany in the Modern Novel* (University of Washington Press, 1971)

———— (ed.), *Critical Essays on Virginia Woolf* (G.K. Hall, 1985)

Bell, C.B., and Ohmann, C., 'Virginia Woolf's Criticism: A Polemical Preface' in (ed.) J. Donovan, *Feminist Literary Criticism: Explorations in Theory* (University Press of Kentucky, 1975)

Bell, Q., *Bloomsbury* (Weidenfeld & Nicolson, 1968)

—————— *Virginia Woolf: A Biography*, 2 vols (Hogarth, 1972)

—————— 'Bloomsbury and the "Vulgar Passions" ', *Critical Inquiry* (Winter, 1979) pp. 239-56

—————— 'Virginia Woolf's Politics', *Virginia Woolf Miscellany* No. 20 (Spring 1983)

—————— 'Who's Afraid for Virginia Woolf?', *New York Review* (15 March 1990), pp. 3-5

Bishop, E., 'The Shaping of Jacob's Room: Woolf's Manuscript Revisions', *Twentieth Century Literature* 32 (1986), pp. 115-35

—————— *A Virginia Woolf Chronology* (Macmillan, 1989)

Black, N., 'Virginia Woolf and the Women's Movement' in *(ed.) J. Marcus (1983)

Blanchot, M., 'Outwitting the Demon', in *The Sirens' Song* (Harvester, 1982)

Bond, A.H., *Who Killed Virginia Woolf? A Psychobiography* (Human Sciences Press, 1989)

Bowlby, R., *Virginia Woolf: Feminist Destinations* (Blackwell, 1988); extract in *(ed.) Su Reid, *New Casebook*

Bradbury, M., *The Modern World: Ten Great Writers* (Penguin, 1989)

—————— and McFarlane, J. (eds), *Modernism: 1890-1930* (Penguin, 1976)

Brewster, D., *Virginia Woolf's London* (George Allen & Unwin, 1959)

Clements, P., and Grundy, I., *Virginia Woolf: New Critical Essays* (USA: Barnes & Noble; UK: Vision Press, 1983)

Cohn, D., *Transparent Minds: Narrative Modes for Presenting Consciousness in Fiction* (Princeton University Press, 1978)

Daiches, D., *Virginia Woolf* (New Directions, 1942; rev. edn, 1963)

—————— *The Novel and the Modern World* (University of Chicago Press, 1960)

Daugherty, B.R., 'The Whole Contention Between Mr Bennett and Mrs Woolf Revisited' in *(eds) E. Ginsberg and L. Gottlieb (1983)

DeSalvo, L., *Virginia Woolf's First Voyage: A Novel in the Making* (Macmillan, 1980)

—————— *Virginia Woolf: The Impact of Childhood Sexual Abuse on her Life and Work* (USA: Beacon Press; UK: Women's Press, 1989)

――――― and Leaska, M. (eds), *The Letters of Vita Sackville-West to Virginia Woolf* (Hutchinson, 1984)

DiBattista, M., *Virginia Woolf's Major Novels: The Fables of Anon* (Yale University Press, 1980)

――――― 'Joyce, Woolf and the Modern Mind' in *(eds) P. Clements and I. Grundy (1983), pp. 96-114

Dowling, D., *Bloomsbury Aesthetics and the Novels of Forster and Woolf* (Macmillan, 1985)

Dunn, J., *A Very Close Conspiracy* (Jonathan Cape, 1990)

Eagleton, M. (ed.), *Feminist Literary Theory: A Reader* (Blackwell, 1986)

Eagleton, T., *Exiles and Emigrés: Studies in Modern Literature* (Schocken, 1970)

Edel, L., *Bloomsbury: A House of Lions* (Hogarth, 1979)

Eisenberg, N., 'Virginia Woolf's Last Words: *Between the Acts* and "Anon" ' in *(ed.) J. Marcus (1981), pp. 253-266

Empson, W., '*Mrs Dalloway* as a Political Satire' in *Argufying* (Chatto & Windus, 1987)

Fleishman, A., *Virginia Woolf: A Critical Reading* (Johns Hopkins University Press, 1975)

―――― 'Forms of the Woolfian Short Story' in *(ed.) R. Freedman (1980)

Flint, K., 'Virginia Woolf and the General Strike', *Essays in Criticism* 36 (1986), pp. 319-34

Freedman, R. (ed.), *Virginia Woolf: Revaluation and Continuity* (University of California Press, 1980)

Friedman, M., 'The Symbolist Novel: Huysmans to Malraux' in *(eds) J. Bradbury and M. McFarlane (1976)

Gillespie, D.F., *The Sisters' Arts: The Writing and Painting of Virginia Woolf and Vanessa Bell* (Syracuse University Press, 1988)

Gindin, J., 'Method in the Biographical Study of Virginia Woolf', *Biography*, vol. 4 (1981) pp. 95-107

Ginsberg, E.K., and Gottlieb, L.M. (eds), *Virginia Woolf: Centennial Essays* (Whitston, 1983)

Goldensohn, L., 'Unburying the Statue: The Lives of Virginia Woolf', *Salmagundi* No.74-5 (Spring/Summer 1987), pp. 1-41

Goldman, M., *The Reader's Art: Virginia Woolf as Literary Critic* (Mouton, 1976)

Gordon, L., 'Our Silent Life: Virginia Woolf and T.S. Eliot' in *(eds) P. Clements and I. Grundy (1983), pp. 77-95

――――― *Virginia Woolf: A Writer's Life* (Oxford University Press, 1986)

Gottlieb, L.M., 'The Years: A Feminist Novel' in *(eds) E.K. Ginsberg and L.M. Gottlieb (1983)

Graham, J., 'The "Caricature Value" of Parody and Fantasy in Orlando' in *(ed.) C. Sprague (1971)

Griffin, G., 'Braving the Mirror: Virginia Woolf as Autobiographer', *Biography*, vol. 4 (1981) pp. 108-18

Guiguet, J., *Virginia Woolf and her Works* (Hogarth, 1965)

———— (ed.), *Contemporary Writers* (Hogarth Press, 1965)

Hafley, J., *The Glass Roof* (Russell & Russell, 1954; repr. 1963)

———— 'Virginia Woolf's Narrators and the Art of "Life Itself"' in *(ed.) R. Freedman (1980)

Haller, E., 'The Anti-Madonna in the Work and Thought of Virginia Woolf' in *(eds) E.K. Ginsberg and L.M. Gottlieb (1983)

Harper, H., *Between Language and Silence: The Novels of Virginia Woolf* (Louisiana State University Press, 1982)

Hartman, G., 'Virginia's Web' in *Beyond Formalism* (Yale University Press, 1970)

Hawkes, E., 'The Virgin in the Bell Biography', *Twentieth Century Literature* 20 (1974), pp. 96-113

———— 'Woolf's "Magical Garden of Women"' in *(ed.) Jane Marcus (1981)

Hawthorn, J., *Virginia Woolf's 'Mrs Dalloway': A Study in Alienation* (Chatto & Windus for Sussex University Press, 1975)

Heilbrun, C., *Towards Androgyny: Aspects of Male and Female in Literature* (Gollancz, 1973)

———— *Writing a Woman's Life* (Norton, 1988)

Henig, S., 'Ulysses in Bloomsbury', *James Joyce Quarterly* 10 (1973), pp. 203-8

Henke, S., 'Mrs Dalloway: the Communion of Saints' in *(ed.) Jane Marcus (1981)

———— 'Virginia Woolf Reads James Joyce: the Ulysses Notebook' in (eds) M. Beja, et. al., *James Joyce: The Centennial Symposium* (University of Illinois Press, 1986)

Hill, K., 'Virginia Woolf and Leslie Stephen: History and Literary Revolution', *Proceedings of the Modern Languages Association* 96 (1981), pp. 351-62 and 97 (1982), pp.103-4

Hochman, B., *The Test of Character from the Victorian Novel to the Modern* (Associated University Presses, 1983)

Hoffman, C., 'From Short Story to Novel: The Manuscript Revisions of Virginia Woolf's *Mrs Dalloway*', *Modern Fiction Studies* 14 (1968), pp. 171-86

Holroyd, M., *Lytton Strachey and the Bloomsbury Group* (Penguin, 1971)
——— 'Virginia Woolf: An Unsuitable Case for Biography?' in *Unreceived Opinions* (Penguin, 1976)
——— 'Bloomsbury and the Fabians' in *(ed.) J. Marcus (1987)

Holtby, W., *Virginia Woolf: A Critical Memoir* (Wishart, 1932)

Homans, M., *Bearing the Word: Language and Female Experience in Nineteenth Century Women's Writing* (Chicago University Press, 1986); extract in *(ed.) Su Reid, *New Casebook*

Hummel, M., 'From the Common Reader to the Uncommon Critic: *Three Guineas* and the Epistolary Form', *Bulletin of the New York Public Library* 80 (1977)

Hussey, M., *The Singing of the Real World: The Philosophy of Virginia Woolf's Fiction* (Ohio State University Press, 1986)
——— (ed.), *Virginia Woolf and War: Fiction, Reality and Myth* (Syracuse University Press, 1992)

Hynes, S., 'The "Whole Contention" Between Mr Bennett and Mrs Woolf' in *Edwardian Occasions: Essays on English Writing in the Early Twentieth Century* (Oxford University Press, 1972)

Johnson, P., 'From Virginia Woolf to the Post-Moderns: Developments in a Feminist Aesthetic', *Radical Philosophy*, No. 45 (Spring 1987), repr. in (eds) S. Sayers, and P. Osborne, *Socialism, Feminism and Philosophy* (Routledge, 1990)

Johnstone, J.K., *The Bloomsbury Group: A Study of E.M. Forster, Lytton Strachey, Virginia Woolf and their Circle* (Secker & Warburg, 1954)

Kennedy, R., *A Boy at the Hogarth Press* (Penguin, 1978)

Keynes, J.M., 'My Early Beliefs' in (ed.) D. Garnett, *Two Memoirs* (Rupert Hart-Davies, 1949), repr. in *(ed.) S.P. Rosenbaum (1975)

Kirkpatrick, B.J., *A Bibliography of Virginia Woolf*, 3rd edn (Oxford University Press, 1980)

Latham, J., 'The Manuscript revisions of Virginia Woolf's *Mrs Dalloway*: A Postscript', *Modern Fiction Studies* 18 (1972), pp. 475-6

Lawrence, K., 'Gender and Narrative Voice in *Jacob's Room* and *A Portrait of the Artist as a Young Man*' in (eds) M. Beja, et. al, *James Joyce: The Centennial Symposium* (University of Illinois Press, 1986)

Leaska, M., *Virginia Woolf's Lighthouse: A Study in Critical Method* (Hogarth, 1970)

———— *The Novels of Virginia Woolf from Beginning to End* (USA: John Jay Press; UK: Weidenfeld & Nicolson, 1977)

Lee, H., *The Novels of Virginia Woolf* (Methuen, 1977)

Lehmann, J., *Virginia Woolf* (Thames & Hudson, 1975)

Lewis, T., ' "Combining the Advantages of Fact and Fiction": Virginia Woolf's Biographies of Vita Sackville-West, Flush and Roger Fry' in *(eds) E.K. Ginsberg and L.M. Gottlieb (1983)

Little, J., *Comedy and the Woman Writer: Woolf, Spark and Feminism* (University of Nebraska Press, 1983)

Lodge, D., *Modes of Modern Writing: Metaphor, Metonymy, and the Typology of Modern Literature* (Edward Arnold, 1977); extract in *(ed.) Su Reid, *New Casebook*

Love, J.O., *Virginia Woolf: Sources of Madness and Art* (University of California Press, 1977)

MacKay, C.H., 'The Thackeray Connection: Virginia Woolf's Aunt Anny', in *(ed.) J. Marcus (1987)

McLaurin, A., *Virginia Woolf: The Echoes Enslaved* (Cambridge University Press, 1973)

———— 'Consciousness and Group Consciousness in Virginia Woolf' in *(ed.) E. Warner (1984)

McNichol, S., *Virginia Woolf and the Poetry of Fiction* (Routledge, Chapman & Hall, 1990)

Majumdar, R., *Virginia Woolf: An Annotated Bibliography of Criticism 1915-1974* (Garland, 1976)

———— and McLaurin, A., *Virginia Woolf: The Critical Heritage* (Routledge & Kegan Paul, 1975)

Marcus, J., 'The Years as Greek Drama, Domestic Novel and Götterdämmerung', *Bulletin of the New York Public Library* 80 (1977)

———— (ed.), *New Feminist Essays on Virginia Woolf* (USA: University of Nebraska Press; UK: Macmillan, 1981)

———— (ed.), *Virginia Woolf: A Feminist Slant* (University of Nebraska Press, 1983)

———— (ed.), *Virginia Woolf and Bloomsbury: A Centenary Celebration* (Macmillan, 1987)

———— *Art and Anger: Reading Like a Woman* (Ohio State University Press for Miami University, 1988)

———— *Virginia Woolf and the Languages of Patriarchy* (Indiana University Press, 1988)

Marder, H., *Feminism and Art: A Study of Virginia Woolf* (University of Chicago Press, 1968)

Matro, T., 'Only Relations: Vision and Achievement in *To the Lighthouse*', *Proceedings of the Modern Languages Association* 99 (1984), pp. 212-24

Mauron, C., *The Nature of Beauty in Art and Literature* (Hogarth, 1927)

Meisel, P., *The Absent Father: Virginia Woolf and Walter Pater* (Yale University Press, 1980)

Mepham, J., 'Figures of Desire: Narration and Fiction in *To the Lighthouse*' in (ed.) G. Josipovici *The Modern English Novel: The Reader, the Writer and the Work* (Open Books, 1976); extract in *(ed.) Su Reid, *New Casebook*

———— 'Trained to Silence', *London Review of Books* (3 December 1980)

———— 'Mourning and Modernism' in *(eds) C. Clements and I. Grundy (1983)

———— *Virginia Woolf: A Literary Life* (Macmillan, 1991)

Meyerowitz, S., 'What is to Console Us? The Politics of Deception in Woolf's Short Stories' in *(ed.) J. Marcus (1981), pp. 238-252

Meyers, J., *Katherine Mansfield: A Biography* (Hamish Hamilton, 1978)

Miller, J.H., *Fiction and Repetition: Seven English Novels* (Blackwell, 1982); extract in *(ed.) Su Reid, *New Casebook*

Miller, N. (ed.), *The Poetics of Gender* (Columbia University Press, 1986)

Minow-Pinkney, M., *Virginia Woolf and the Problem of the Subject* (Harvester, 1987); extract in *(ed.) Su Reid, *New Casebook*

Moi, T., *Sexual/Textual Politics: Feminist Literary Theory* (Methuen, 1985); extract in *(ed.) Su Reid, *New Casebook*

Moore, M., (ed.), 'Virginia Woolf's *Orlando*: an Edition of the Manuscript', *Twentieth Century Literature* 25 (1979) pp. 303-46

———— *The Short Season Between Two Silences: The Mystical and the Political in the Novels of Virginia Woolf* (George Allen & Unwin, 1984)

Morgenstern, B., 'The Self-Conscious Narrator in *Jacob's Room*', *Modern Fiction Studies* 18 (1972), pp. 351f.

Naremore, J., *The World Without a Self: Virginia Woolf and the Novel* (Yale University Press, 1973)

Nicolson, N., *Portrait of a Marriage* (Weidenfeld & Nicolson, 1973)

Noble, J.R., *Recollections of Virginia Woolf* (Penguin, 1975)

Poole. R., *The Unknown Virginia Woolf* (Cambridge University Press, 1978; new edn, Harvester, 1982)

Radin, G., *Virginia Woolf's 'The Years': The Evolution of a Novel* (The University of Tennessee Press, 1981)

Reid, S. (ed.), *The Critics Debate 'To the Lighthouse'*, (Macmillan, 1991)

———— (ed.), *Mrs Dalloway and To the Lighthouse: A New Casebook* (Macmillan, forthcoming)

Rice, T., *Virginia Woolf: A Guide to Research* (Garland, 1984)

Richter, H., *Virginia Woolf: The Inward Voyage* (Princeton University Press, 1970)

Ricoeur, P., *Time and Narrative*, vol. 2 (University of Chicago Press, 1985)

Rose. P., *Woman of Letters: A Life of Virginia Woolf* (Routledge & Kegan Paul, 1978)

———— *Writing of Women: Essays in a Renaissance* (Wesleyan University Press, 1985)

Rosenbaum, S.P. (ed.), *The Bloomsbury Group: A Collection of Memoirs, Commentary and Criticism* (University of Toronto Press, 1975)

———— 'An Educated Man's Daughter: Leslie Stephen, Virginia Woolf and the Bloomsbury Group' in *(eds) P. Clements and I. Grundy (1983), pp. 32-56

———— 'Virginia Woolf and the Intellectual Origins of Bloomsbury' in *(eds) E.K. Ginsberg and L.M. Gottlieb (1983)

———— *Victorian Bloomsbury: The Early Literary History of the Bloomsbury Group*, vol. 1 (Macmillan, 1987)

Rosenthal, M., *Virginia Woolf* (Routledge & Kegan Paul, 1979)

Ruddick, S., 'Private Brother, Public World' in * (ed.) J. Marcus (1981), pp. 185-215

Ruotolo, L., *The Interrrupted Moment: A View of Virginia Woolf's Novels* (Stanford University Press, 1986)

Schaefer, J.O., 'The Vision Falters: *The Years*, 1937' in *(ed.) C. Sprague (1971)

Schlack, B.A., 'Virginia Woolf's Strategy of Scorn in *The Years* and *Three Guineas*', *Bulletin of the New York Public Library* 80 (1977)

———— *Continuing Presences: Virginia Woolf's Use of Literary Allusion* (Pennsylvania State University Press, 1979)

Shattuck, S.D., 'The Stage of Scholarship: Crossing the Bridge from Harrison to Woolf' in *(ed.) J. Marcus (1987), pp. 287-98

Showalter, E., *A Literature of Their Own: British Women Novelists From Brontë to Lessing* (Virago, 1978)

Silver, B., '*Three Guineas* Before and After: Further Answers to Correspondents' in *(ed.) J. Marcus (1983)

———— *Virginia Woolf's Reading Notebooks* (Princeton University Press, 1983)

Smith, C., '*Three Guineas*: Virginia Woolf's Prophecy' *(ed.) J. Marcus (1987), pp. 225-41

Spalding, F., *Vanessa Bell* (Weidenfeld & Nicolson, 1983)

Spater, G., and Parsons, I., *A Marriage of True Minds: An Intimate Portrait of Leonard and Virginia Woolf* (Jonathan Cape & Hogarth, 1977)

Spilka, M., 'New Life in the Works: Some Recent Woolf Studies', *Novel* 12 (1979) pp. 169-84

———— *Virginia Woolf's Quarrel with Grieving* (University of Nebraska Press, 1980)

Spivak, G.C., 'Unmaking and Making in *To the Lighthouse*' in *In Other Worlds: Essays in Cultural Politics* (Methuen, 1987)

Sprague, C. (ed.), *Virginia Woolf: A Collection of Critical Essays* (Prentice-Hall, 1971)

Squier, S.M., ' "The Track of Our Own": Typescript drafts of *The Years*', *Modernist Studies: Literature and Culture 1920-1940*, vol. 4 (1982) pp. 218-31, also in *(ed.) J. Marcus (1983), pp.198-211

———— *Virginia Woolf and London: The Sexual Politics of the City* (University of North Carolina Press, 1985)

Steele, E., *Virginia Woolf's Literary Sources and Allusions* (Garland, 1983)

Steinberg, E. (ed.), *The Stream-of-Consciousness Technique in the Modern Novel* (Kennikat Press, 1979)

Stemerick, M., 'The Madonna's Clay Feet' in *(ed.) J. Marcus (1983)

———— 'Virginia Woolf and Julia Stephen: The Distaff Side of History' in *(eds) E.K. Ginsberg and L.M. Gottlieb (1983)

Stubbs, P., *Women and Fiction: Feminism and the Novel 1880-1920* (Harvester, 1979)

Szladits, L., ' The Life, Character and Opinions of Flush the Spaniel', *Bulletin of the New York Public Library* 74 (1970), pp. 211-18

Thickstun, W.R., *Visionary Closure in the Modern Novel* (Macmillan, 1988)

Transue, P., *Virginia Woolf and the Politics of Style* (SUNY Press, 1986)

Trautmann, J., *The Jessamy Brides: The Friendship of Virginia Woolf and V. Sackville-West* (Pennsylvania State University Press, 1973); extract in *(ed.) M. Beja (1985), pp. 97-106

Trombley, S., '*All that Summer She Was Mad*': *Virginia Woolf and Her Doctors* (Junction Books, 1981)

Warner, E. (ed.), *Virginia Woolf: A Centenary Perspective* (Macmillan, 1984)

———— *Virginia Woolf: 'The Waves'* (Cambridge University Press, 1987)

Watney, S., 'The Connoisseur as Gourmet: The Aesthetics of Roger Fry and Clive Bell' in (eds) T. Bennett, *et. al.*, *Formations of Pleasure* (Routledge & Kegan Paul, 1983)

Weiser, B., 'Criticism of Virginia Woolf From 1956 to the Present: A Selected Checklist With an Index to Studies of Separate Works', *Modern Fiction Studies* 18 (1972), pp. 477-86

Wheare, J., *Virginia Woolf: Dramatic Novelist* (Macmillan, 1989)

Williams, R., *The Country and the City* (Chatto & Windus, 1973)

———— 'The Bloomsbury Fraction', *Problems in Materialism and Culture* (Verso, 1980)

Wilson, J.J., 'Why is *Orlando* Difficult?' in *(ed.) J. Marcus (1981), pp. 170-84

Woolf, L., *An Autobiography*, 2 vols (Oxford University Press, 1980)

Yeazell, R.B., 'Doctors' Orders', *London Review of Books* (18 February 1982)

Zwerdling, A., *Virginia Woolf and the Real World* (University of California Press, 1986)

Kettle, Arnold, 25
Keynes, Maynard, 34, 35, 36
Kierkegaard, 40, 94
Kirkpatrick, B.J., 21, 23
Klein, Melanie, 32
Kristeva, Julia, 2, 70, 71, 72, 73, 77

Labour Party, 29
Lacan, 2, 69, 70, 77
Laing, R.D., 14
Langer, Susanne, 92
Latham, J., 101
Lawrence, D.H., 35, 36, 40, 49, 64, 94
Lawrence, Karen, 110
Leaska, Mitchell, 5, 6, 100, 112, 114, 115
Leavis, Q.D., 22, 64
Lee, Hermione, 2, 98, 99, 100, 112
Lehmann, John, 13
Lewis, Thomas. 117
Little, Judy, 84, 85, 110
Lodge, David, 31, 45, 46, 47, 100, 112
Love, J.O., 8, 13, 16, 17, 19

MacKay, C.H., 38
McFarlane, 43, 81
McLaurin, Allen, 21, 22, 40, 94, 107, 113
McNeillie, Andrew, 5, 116
McNichol, Stella, 103, 104, 111
Majumdar, Robin, 21, 22, 24
Mallarmé 73
Malraux, 44
Mann, Thomas, 52
Mansfield, Katherine, 21, 46, 82
Marcus, Jane, 2, 8, 9, 26, 35, 38, 59, 68, 108, 110, 114

Marder, Herbert, 68, 78, 79, 80
Matro, Thomas, 41, 42
Mauron, Charles, 39, 40
Meisel, Perry, 38, 116
Mepham, John, 2, 11, 12, 19, 22, 32, 37, 104, 112, 118
Meredith, 84
Merleau-Ponty, 14, 89, 94
Meyerounts, Selma, 115
Meyers, Jeffrey, 46
Miller, John Hillis, 94, 95, 108, 111
Miller, Nancy, 59
Minow-Pinkney, Makiko, 2, 69, 70, 71, 72, 73, 74, 75, 76, 111, 112
Moi, Toril, 72, 73, 79, 103
Moments of Being, 6, 9, 34, 117
Monday or Tuesday, 115
Moore, G.E., 35, 37, 48
Moore, Madeline, 66, 67, 112
Morgenstern, Barry, 110
Mrs Dalloway, 12, 13, 16, 18, 27, 30, 31, 44, 46, 47, 56, 62, 67, 80, 82, 84, 90, 94, 95, 96, 103, 110, 111, 115
Muir, Edwin, 22

Naremore, James, 2, 55, 106, 107, 108
Nicolson, Harold, 112
Nicolson, Nigel, 13
Night and Day, 15, 69, 78, 80, 82, 83, 85, 100, 102, 106, 110
Noble, Jean Russell, 13

Ohmann, 117
Orlando, 22, 61, 62, 67, 75, 85, 100, 112

Parsons, 12

Pater, Walter, 38, 116
Poole, Roger, 2, 8, 13, 14, 15, 16, 17, 19, 37, 38
Proust, M., 48, 52, 53

Radin, Grace, 114
Raverat, Jacques, 39
Reid, Su, 111, 112
Rice, Thomas, 24
Rich, Adrienne, 82
Richardson, Dorothy, 21, 40, 53, 65
Richter, Harvena, 37, 55, 92, 104, 108
Ricoeur, Paul, 96, 111
Rose, Phyllis, 2, 9, 13, 19, 26, 61, 79, 80, 81, 108, 117, 118
Rosenbaum, S.P., 37, 113
Rosenthal, Michael, 104, 108
Ruddick, Sara, 27, 58, 59, 107, 110
Ruotolo, Lucio, 105

Sackville-West, Vita, 13, 67, 112
Sartre, J-P., 87, 89
Schaefer, J.O., 114
Schlack, Beverly Ann, 23, 24, 68
Scott, Walter, 101
Second World War, 53
Shakespeare, Judith, 65, 83
Shakespeare, William, 95
Shattuck, S.D., 38
Showalter, Elaine, 62, 63, 64, 65, 73, 102, 103
Silver, Brenda, 24, 68, 115
Smith, Catherine, 68
Spalding, Frances, 35
Spark, Muriel, 84
Spater, G., 12
Spender, Stephen, 22
Spilka, Mark, 13, 17, 18, 19, 81

Spivak, Gayatri Chakravorty, 96
Sprague, C., 108
Squier, Susan Merrill, 82, 83, 84, 102, 108, 110, 113, 114
Steele, Elizabeth, 23
Steinberg, Erwin, 50, 53, 54, 55
Stemerick, Martine, 13
Stephen, Adrian, 32
Stephen, Caroline Emilia, 9, 38
Stephen, Karin, 32
Stephen, Leslie, 13
Sterne, 84
Storm Jameson, 22
Strachey, Lytton, 34
Stubbs, Patricia, 64, 65, 102, 103
Szladits, 113

Thackeray, Anny, 38
The Pargiters, 63, 102, 113
The Voyage Out, 15, 17, 21, 45, 69, 80, 85, 90, 100, 102, 103, 106, 110, 113
The Waves, 11, 12, 45, 47, 56, 57, 80, 89, 91, 92, 101, 103, 105, 106, 112, 113
The Years, 12, 18, 22, 63, 67, 68, 69, 78, 79, 80, 84, 100, 102, 103, 113, 114
Thickstun, W.R., 48, 49
Three Guineas, 22, 28, 33, 36, 59, 60, 63, 66, 67, 68, 69, 80, 84, 102, 114
To the Lighthouse, 12, 18, 22, 27, 29, 33, 41, 47, 49, 50, 51, 56, 61, 75, 77, 78, 79, 80, 91, 92, 94, 95, 96, 97, 99, 100, 104, 105, 111, 112
Transue, Pamela, 103, 114
Trautmann, Joanne, 9, 108, 112
Trombley, Stephen 16, 113

Warner, Eric, 108, 113
Watney, S., 39
Watt, Dr Isaac, 96
Weiser, Barbara, 24
West, Rebecca, 82
Wheare, Jane, 65, 100, 101, 102, 103, 114
Williams, Raymond, 29, 35, 82
Wilson, J.J., 112

Wolfe, Thomas, 47
Wollstonecraft, Mary, 65
Woolf, Leonard, 5, 8, 14, 15, 16, 21, 34, 35, 36, 37, 116

Yeazell, R.B., 16

Zwerdling, Alex, 2, 25, 26, 27, 28, 32, 44, 81